MANAGING BUSINESS NETWORKS

MANAGING BUSINESS NETWORKS

A Practical Guide to Starting and Running Them

TIM KIDD

KOGAN PAGE

To my most important network — my family

First published in 1994

Kogan Page Limited
120 Pentonville Road
London N1 9JN

British Library Cataloguing-in-Publication Data

A CIP record for this book is available from the British Library.

ISBN 0 7494 1014 0

Typeset by Photoprint, Torquay, Devon
Printed and bound in Great Britain by Clays Ltd, St Ives plc

Contents

Acknowledgements

I started this book when I was working at City and Inner London North Training and Enterprise Council (CILN-TEC). My challenge at CILNTEC was to establish a Management Charter Initiative (MCI) Network. I therefore owe much to my friends at CILNTEC and MCI for the ideas and opportunities that they so freely offered.

1: What is a business network?

There is nothing new about networks. St Paul set up a very successful one which is still going strong. Winnie the Pooh was ruthless in exploiting his network when it was time for a little something. And the three witches in *Macbeth* were clearly strong networkers as they gathered round their cauldron and croissants screeching 'When shall we three meet again?'

You may think you already know what a network is, and some readers may be tempted to slope off to the end of this chapter and wait for the rest of us to catch up. But, given their long history, and the current popularity of networks of the 'power breakfast' variety, it would be foolish to assume we all share the same definition of a network. So let us explore the essential characteristics, and consign some unwanted undergrowth to the compost heap.

THE LITERAL MEANING OF 'NETWORK'

Dr Johnson's definition of *network* in his 1755 Dictionary has long been used as an example of how to make obscure a thing which is in itself very plain: 'Any thing reticulated or decussated at equal distances, with interstices between the intersections.'

The literal meaning of *network* according to the Oxford English Dictionary is, thank goodness, not such heavy going: 'a work in which threads, wires or similar materials are arranged in the fashion of a net.'

The figurative uses of network

For several hundreds of years the term has been used figuratively in many different ways, so that although we recognise a circus safety net when we see one, if we use network as a metaphor or simile then our common understanding seems to fall right through Dr Johnson's interstices.

When you saw this book's title, you may have expected all sorts of different networks to be covered, so let me tell you right away what this book is *not* about, and what I will consign to my compost heap immediately:

1. A system of cables for the distribution of electricity or television programmes. Although this is called a network, it only currently permits one-way traffic, and one of the aspects of business networks that I will be emphasising in a later chapter is the importance of two-way traffic in measuring the network's effectiveness.

2. A diagram of interconnected events or processes as

used in the study of work efficiency. Thus a network diagram could be used to represent all the events which will have to happen before you can relocate a business from one part of the country to another.

Although I have only mentioned this use of the word in order to discard it, I would like to draw attention to an important rule of network analysis which is that every line (or event) must connect with something else on the diagram, and it must represent an event which is significant for the project. This is an important discipline which can be applied to the management of a business network. If your job is to set up a network then you should be able to demonstrate the significance of each strand or bridge between members.

3. Computer terminal configurations, often described as Local Area Networks (LANs) or Wide Area Networks (WANs). However, I am not going to leave this aspect of networks without an admission of envy for the ability of the LAN and WAN controllers to be able to monitor the use of the network by the various terminals. As I will be suggesting later, the network manager (in my sense of the term) should be encouraging network members to interact with each other as well as the manager, but there is, as yet, no easy way to monitor this interaction.

   It is also an area where business network managers can learn valuable lessons from the computer network managers, who are confronted by the problem of increasing levels of 'downtime' as computer networks become larger and more complex. Part of the problem is that most users spend less than 5 per cent of their information technology budget on network management, whereas 10–15 per cent would allow users to lay down basic network requirements and monitor any events that may put those targets at risk. Business network managers should also set targets for performance, and I deal with objective setting in Chapter Three.

4. A complex collection or system of rivers, canals or railways.

Mention of the railways brings me abruptly up against the buffers. I can now define what sort of network this book describes. A railway network requires two sorts of manager. One is a 'Fat Controller' who is required to maintain the fabric of the network. Someone has to superintend the building of the rail system and the maintenance of the track and stations. In this book, I want to draw a distinction between this type of management — let us call it *fabric management* — and managing the associated *business network* which concerns the relationship between the railway owners and all the different organisations who have some interest in the rail network. A rail network which is maintained perfectly in the fabric management sense will not survive for long without customers for its services. Bringing in the revenue requires a business network manager, and this book is all about setting up and managing a business network. A business network is a network of organisations or individuals who combine, perhaps only intermittently, to achieve specific business objectives.

Although I will be concentrating on the business

network, in practice it may not be easy always to show where fabric management ends and business network management begins. In the debate about rail privatisation, control of the tracks by franchisees is high on the agenda, so fabric management and business network management have become closely linked.

Many business networks of course have no assets other than a supply of headed notepaper, so for them there is no fabric management, only business network management.

Grammarians will have spotted that network has so far been used as a noun, but it is now also used as a verb — *to network*.

The cutting edge of the word has been blunted by overuse, so now it can be used to describe, and often to confer an unjustified importance on, attendance at any social function: 'If anyone wants me, I'll be down at the pub, networking.' Some writers have tried to rescue the word from its degradation, and re-sharpen it. Anne Boe and Bettie B Youngs set out a list of examples of what networking is in *Is your 'net' working?* (John Wiley & Sons, 1989). Apparently networking includes 'loving yourself enough to love and give to others' (back to St Paul!) and 'the ability to make all your dreams come true' (back to *Macbeth*!).

For a more prosaic definition, we can turn to the Management Charter Initiative (MCI), who offer:

> making and maintaining a variety of contacts with people and groups both inside and outside the organisation, getting known and becoming recognised as someone who has a worthwhile contribution to make.

Figure 1.1 The 'Old Boy Network'
(This cartoon appears courtesy of the *Oldie* magazine)

CHECKLIST

- What are the four types of network not covered in this book?
- What is the definition of a business network?

The brainshaker question is:
What was Dr Johnson's definition of network?

2: Why do business networks need managers?

Vanishing managers

Management used to be built in to many business networks, simply because everyone in the network belonged to the same organisation. The management framework was in place.

Then came the early nineties 'ice age', when many management jobs became extinct. IBM UK, for example, eroded four of their eight layers of management.

In-house goes out

At the same time as the managers were being winnowed the organisations were being threshed, and all but the core functions were blown away by the chill wind of change.

The BBC introduced 'Producer Choice', which allowed producers to buy services from non-BBC providers. Forty-five dressers at BBC Television lost their jobs when their function of looking after and laundering costumes was contracted out. IBM UK has turned its headquarters functions into service units, and the other parts of the company can use them if they wish. If they don't wish. . . .

Let's look at these two significant developments to see what the implications are for network management.

Networks are not new, but in the pre-glacial era there was enough management time available for someone to manage them. The network's objectives were, or should have been, consistent with the organisation's objectives. Under the old 'in-house' arrangements, when purchasers and providers of services all worked for the same organisation, the network would have been managed, but it would probably not have been identified as 'network management' in anybody's job description. The classic human resource management functions of recruiting, retaining and motivating the network members would have formed part of a specific person's task.

HOW HAVE THINGS CHANGED?

The current challenge is to break through departmental barriers to prevent innovation being slowed or even stifled by bureaucracy. Terms like process re-engineering or core process redesign are still battling for supremacy, but what the terms mean essentially is ditching the belief that specialisation and compartmentalisation are the best ways to get things done on a grand scale. Central planning and a mechanistic approach do not work. Come back Jack (and of course Jill) of all trades!

See, for example, this statement in the Norsk Hydro Annual Report for 1991:

> The organisational challenge of the 90s will be to continue to develop a decentralised decision-making system and at the same time preserve Norsk Hydro as a strong and uniform concern. The company will therefore aim, among other things, to utilise more fully the extensive professional competence in related fields existing within the company, across the traditional business areas.

As these new business networks are established, the first question must always be: *Who is managing the business network?*

Organisations like Norsk Hydro can no longer afford to seek all the answers from within the organisation though, and the Annual Report says:

> In addition to strengthening the company's own technological competence, Hydro wishes to develop further its cooperation in research and technology with universities, institutes, and suppliers in and outside Norway. In this context particular attention is being given to the EC.

Co-operate, don't dominate

Of course, Norsk Hydro is not alone. A report by Michyo Nakamoto in the *Financial Times* about Japanese investment in the EC characterised R&D investment as the *third wave*. The first wave was investment in basic assembly facilities; the second was investment in component suppliers. The difference with the third wave is that it involves collaborative efforts rather than wholly-owned subsidiaries. If you like to collect Japanese management phrases, then you should note down 'Kyo-sei', which means global symbiotic cooperation!

This move from a business network based on an owner-subsidiary relationship to a collaborator-based business network is not confined to Japanese companies. One example is IBM, which is in the process of splitting into a loose network of separate business units. Another example is ICI. As long ago as 1950 a committee of ICI directors was asking whether the company should not be split up. They foresaw that a single board of directors might not be able to give sufficiently close and knowledgeable attention to all ICI's investment decisions. At its peak, these decisions involved processes ranging from chlorine manufacture to seed breeding. Either their foresight was remarkable, or their proposals for major changes encountered strong resistance, for it was not until 1993 that ICI spun off much the biggest part of its business to form Zeneca.

Once again we have to ask: *Who is the business network manager?*

The question will need to be asked increasingly often. Just taking the number of Japanese manufacturers in the EC with research and development (R&D) facilities as an example, there has been an increase from 70 in two years to 200 at the beginning of 1992. The timing is beneficial to UK universities which are now turning to business networks to find funds for their research projects. There is also a financial benefit to businesses, who can commission academic institutions to conduct research in areas where they cannot do so themselves because of a lack of facilities or staff. Knowledge-based companies have to change their working practices, and they need to support this by changing their management practices. They will be forced by competitive pressures to improve the abilities of their business network managers.

WHAT ARE THE BENEFITS OF BUSINESS NETWORKS?

The financial benefits of business networks will come back to haunt the end of this chapter, but there are other benefits. The Japanese, for example, are learning about new ways of approaching R&D. According to Michiyo Nakamoto, their approach tends to be evolutionary, whereas in the West the emphasis is on creativity and big, revolutionary breakthroughs. A network avoids one side or the other 'winning' and then imposing its corporate culture on the vanquished.

The question of a takeover may, in any case, be out of the question because of the number of companies that would need to be acquired. Westinghouse Electric, for example, has cooperative agreements with companies in over a dozen other countries, including Rolls Royce in the UK; various Mitsubishi companies in Japan; and FiatAvio in Italy. This means they are plugged into a network of 9000 engineers who are working on turbines. If such a huge 'department' were to be owned by a single company then creativity would probably lose out to bureaucracy.

Another example of blending cultures rather than imposing one common set of values can be seen in the work being done on European television standards by Matsushita, which is based near Frankfurt, and involves a business network including the Universities of Frankfurt and Darmstadt, and the Cologne Academy of Media Arts.

NEW MANAGEMENT SKILLS REQUIRED

This new way of working unsettles many senior managers who see it as a fundamental challenge to their traditional power bases. It requires all the organisation's work processes to be examined and redesigned, but not in isolation. At the same time as an organisation addresses the 'hard' aspects of its operations, it has to redesign the 'soft' aspects. Its formal organisation structure must mirror the new processes; its people have to get the necessary skills to cope with the new multi-disciplinary work practices; and the culture has to change so that people no longer think along departmental tramlines. Informal networks within the organisation, and outside it, will become a vital component of the change, and these networks will have to be properly managed if they are going to deliver.

In her book *The Change Masters* (Unwin, London, 1988), Rosabeth Moss Kanter says there are four kinds of integrative device which can aid network formation in a large organisation:

1. Frequent job moves, including lateral moves, so that people get to know each other and how the organisation works.

2. Employment security. Integration is easier when you work with someone for the greater good rather than compete against them for their job.

3. Extensive use of formal team mechanisms, on the assumption that no individual can know everything, and so people must practise working together.

4. There should be plenty of dotted lines on the

company organogram to show that interdepartmental cooperation is OK.

These devices can only be used in big organisations, of course, but they do give some handy pointers to the sort of job experience that would be handy for a business network manager. There is more about that in Chapter Five.

Benchmarking

Any organisation, big or small, can benefit from learning how others carry out a similar process. The modern management guru's term for poking your nose into other people's business is 'benchmarking'. And it is an activity where efficient network management is essential. Many organisations will find that the obvious targets, their competitors, will be reluctant to join a benchmarking network in order to share all their secrets. The skill of the network manager will therefore lie in identifying and enrolling non-competitors who can nevertheless contribute useful ideas to the benchmarking circle.

An example of this kind of lateral thinking is the National Health Service, when it wanted to examine its procedures for dealing with patients who failed to keep their hospital appointments. They turned for help, via their benchmarking network, to an airline which had considerable experience in dealing with 'non-appearers'.

COUNTING THE COST

Setting up and managing a business network of any kind is not cheap, and anyone wanting to do it should be sure that it is going to contribute to the achievement of competitive advantage. That is why I advocate giving the responsibility to a person or team, with their own budget. Somebody should be accountable for the success of the network.

While the quest for innovation is undoubtedly prompting the formation of many new cross-boundary business networks, the most forceful goal is the prospect of cost reduction. Necessity is the mother of collaboration.

Can business networks make silk purses for cost savings?

Look at almost any set of annual accounts and you will see a few ritual sentences in the chairman's statement about people being the organisation's most valuable resource. But the chairman could just as well have said that people are the most *costly* resource, because staff costs account for such a high percentage of expenditure for so many organisations.

So, for those caught out by the early nineties downturn in the business cycle, the obvious way to achieve rapid savings was to look critically at staffing levels. This exercise has relied heavily on the thesaurus for euphemisms like rationalisation, downsizing, delayering or refocusing, all of which mean getting rid of staff, but in the process new business networks have to be created.

In some cases, the people who leave have been providing services that the organisation has decided it must do without completely. Whether it is coal pits or bank branches, the story is well enough known not to require repetition here. There are other cases, however, when the organisation realises that it does need the service, but no longer for the customary standard working week throughout the year. The obvious answer is to remove the person, or group of people, from the organisation's payroll and hire them back as and when needed at an hourly or daily rate. A time-share rather than a country estate; a fortnight's charter rather than buying a yacht.

COMPETITIVE TENDERING

Local authorities contract out

In 1993, just over 30 per cent of local authority contracts went to private companies rather than to the local authorities' own direct service organisations.

The London Borough of Bromley is a good example. Capita Managed Services, a private sector company, now looks after most of the borough's financial services. This means they will collect council tax, pay the council workers' salaries, and pay housing benefits. 170 council staff have transferred to Capita on their previous terms and conditions, and will now be able to bid for other contracts in the public or private sector. Bromley expects to save £1 million as a result of the change.

For the past five years UK local government has been encouraged to go down this route, with the compulsory competitive tendering (CCT) legislation giving them the necessary impetus. Berkshire is among the leaders in this process, and awards contracts totalling £35 million a year. The following council services are all now open to private sector tendering:

- grounds maintenance
- computer support

- supplies
- cleaning
- school meals
- vehicle maintenance
- architectural design
- quantity surveying
- school music tuition
- staff training
- highway maintenance and emergencies
- forestry.

And there are plans for other services . . . . .

In many cases private contractors who have made successful bids have employed the former council staff, usually on similar conditions of service, as with Bromley's financial services, except that the psychological contract has been radically changed.

Civil servants compete

The UK government's plans to go down a similar route involved 44,000 civil servants competing against outside contractors during 1993. The value of these activities was about £1.5 billion, with another £1–2 billion worth to follow in 1994, the functions including information technology; legal services; accounting services and typing and secretarial services. So far savings have been about 25 per cent of the original cost, even when the contract has been won by the existing providers.

There may still be some squabbling over the alimony which will be paid by the government to its former employees after the divorce. There is some confusion over whether the European Union's Acquired Rights Directive will be able to secure the pay and conditions of workers as they applied when the work was contracted out. However there is no doubt that the government will still harvest substantial savings.

Downsizing's downside

Funds are essential to ensure that new business networks will be properly managed, because the downside of downsizing is that having once tasted the freedom of being freelance, contractors may take their tenders elsewhere. What is happening in network terms is that the links between network members are being loosened. During the economic downturn this may be unimportant because the power resides with the demand side. Furthermore, many contracts are going to the existing workforce, albeit with a different employer's logo on their overalls, so there are no learning curve problems. This convenient arrangement may not survive an economic upturn, and the business network managers of today should be ensuring that they have a strong, close-knit network ready to cope with the future.

To find out more about starting and running a strong business network, read on!

CHECKLIST

- Who is managing your business network?
- Which four devices are used by large organisations to aid network formation?
- What are the pitfalls of downsizing?

The brainshaker question is:
What is the Japanese term for global symbiotic cooperation?

NETWORKING OFFERS THE OPPORTUNITY TO:

- meet others informally to exchange ideas;
- improve existing business relationships and develop new ones;
- develop interpersonal skills, without pressure from within your own organisation;
- learn new things in an empathetic atmosphere;
- sample different ways to achieve the same goal, or tackle a similar problem, without reinventing the wheel or employing a consultant to reinvent it for you;
- pursue job opportunities;
- meet people who would normally be inaccessible in a more formal, hierarchical environment.

Joanne Philip
Manager, LMB Services Limited

3: How to create and manage a business network

In this chapter I am going to draw on my experience as a network manager to look at the nuts and bolts of running a network. We will cover seven aspects in particular:

1. the objectives of the network
2. who do you want in it, with some cautionary remarks about mailing lists
3. a launch event
4. media coverage
5. other network events
6. newsletters
7. other benefits of membership.

OBJECTIVES

As we have seen in Chapter 1, networking is currently very fashionable, and there are many people in networks, and, indeed, people who are managing them, with not the faintest idea of their network's objectives. If you ask why they are members of the network, they will tell you what the members have in common, rather than what the network does. It is hardly a surprise if those networks never achieve much, and if they do achieve anything, it will be by accident!

Why are we here?

A good place to start is to imagine a world in which your network does not exist. Would it matter? Would anyone notice? If the answer to these questions is *yes*, then you are in a good position to set out the objectives of your network. But before you congratulate yourself on a job well done, remember to diarise an opportunity one year hence to review those objectives and decide whether they still apply. How about a secret ballot of the network members to see how many want to continue?

Some networks can be formed to serve a clearly defined group. For example, the Cleveland Chemical Alarm System links Teeside industrial sites where hazardous materials are handled. Also in the network are the Cleveland police and fire brigade. By using personal computer and telex links, all the network members can be informed within two minutes about an accident or emission. There is no doubt who should be in the network, and consequently there are no network members who do not share the common aim of the rest.

NETWORK MANAGER'S INDUCTION COURSE

When I ran induction courses for new MCI network managers, I asked them to list their main objectives for the course. These are the things they most wanted to learn about:

1. To find out what the job involves by discussing it with several experienced network managers.
2. To establish clear objectives for their own networks that would:
   - a state the overall purpose;
   - b indicate the measures of medium-/long-term effectiveness/success;
   - c provide a basis for short-term monitoring of progress.
3. To improve product knowledge.
4. To understand how network management can enhance the other activities that the manager has to do.
5. To discuss common problems with other new network managers.
6. To build up their own network of network managers.
7. To find out what developments are planned for the future.
8. To understand the personal benefits that come from being a network manager.
9. To find out how to be a better network manager.

There is no point in expanding the network because from its inception it had achieved a critical mass.

Getting serious

For many other networks, it is very difficult to achieve a critical mass so that they can be taken seriously. The prime objective in the early days, therefore, is to expand. This is a legitimate objective, but the network manager must set out the purpose of the expansion, and say what size of oak should emerge from the acorn, so that everyone realises when the objective has been achieved. Sometimes the travelling can be such fun that we forget to alight at our destination. Or else we fall asleep, and end up miles from where we want to be.

Smarten up your act

There is a useful mnemonic which can act as a touchstone for your network's objectives. The question to ask is: are they SMART? And S–M–A–R–T stands for:

Specific: If your objectives are too vague, you may be swamped with members who all think the network is for them and will soon become disillusioned, or else wrest control from you. Alternatively you will not get any members at all, because no one thinks the network is aimed at them.

Measurable: If you cannot measure your progress, how will you know how long it will take to get there? It will also help your publicity if you are able to report achievements for your network year by year that mean something to members and non-members alike.

Achievable: As network manager you will only have limited resources. Decide what these are, and do not set objectives which will require more resources than you will ever have. It is better to decide before you embark on the venture what the difficulties are going to be, rather than find out the hard way that you have set yourself, and others, an impossible task.

Reviewable: Always try to allow yourself some latitude, so that if something unexpected happens you can review the objectives and adjust them to take account of the new circumstances. Unless the objectives have been written down, it will be very difficult to do this. It is always painful to accept defeat, so at least make sure you can do something about it.

Time-limited: Many people assume their networks will last for centuries, unless of course their network is helping to find a cure for some dreadful disease. But even if we cannot accept that our network will ever end, we should set objectives that can be achieved in the near future. If we allow ourselves until the last trump to achieve a particular objective, there is the danger that we will fall a victim to Parkinson's law, which is that work expands to fill the time available for its completion. Putting a time limit to objectives also means that we can attack overwhelming tasks by breaking them down into small, manageable components. As the Chinese proverb has it, a journey of a thousand miles must begin with a single step!

Possibly you followed my recommendation at the beginning of this chapter, and imagined a world in which your network did not exist, and decided that no one *would* notice. If that is the case, you undoubtedly have a 'notwork' on your hands, and rather than continue with this chapter, I suggest you move on to the next one for guidance on whether to repair or terminate. In the meantime the rest of us will think about selecting our teams.

WHO DO YOU WANT IN YOUR NETWORK?

If I may take a liberty with Shakespeare's well-known pronouncement, some people are born into networks; some achieve networks; and some have networks thrust upon them. Never mind how you became a network manager, an essential task is to analyse the membership of your network so that you are prepared for any unwelcome developments.

The first question to ask is: what is your potential membership?

Imagine a specific organisation or individual contacting you to ask for details of your network. Would you be pleased or gobsmacked? Why? There is no substitute for written criteria for membership (but remember that objectives should be reviewable, so you can rewrite them). These criteria will give the basic requirements, but you should also have, although maybe not on paper, a list of the gilt-edged members of your network. Who are the sheep, and who are the goats?

Where should you draw the line?

Geographical boundaries can be a useful starting point. When I set up a Management Charter Initiative (MCI) Network in 1991, I thought I had a clear geographical boundary within which to work. In 1989 MCI set itself the (smart) objective of establishing networks in 100 out of the

105 Local Enterprise Company and Training and Enterprise Council areas in the UK.

My network was to be situated in the City and Inner London North Training and Enterprise Council (CILNTEC) area, and therefore encompassed the City of London, Hackney and Islington. However, in 1991 there were no other MCI Networks in London north of the Thames, so I was responding to enquiries from well beyond the CILNTEC boundaries. Indeed, one meeting I addressed had local authority training managers from all of the Greater London boroughs.

This situation only existed temporarily, as during 1992 several other London TECs set up their own MCI Networks. The CILNTEC/MCI Network is therefore an example of one whose geographical coverage contracted. It can be a welcome development for a network manager to have more time available because the area to be covered is shrinking, and in these circumstances especially it is useful to have a list of prestigious members or potential members on whom the extra time can be spent.

Aim at the target

The important thing is to arrive at a target population for your network. In the CILNTEC area, for example, there are 18,000 businesses, and I was able to tell them about MCI once a quarter through the TEC business magazine. This was therefore one of my network's objectives — written communication to all potential network members every quarter.

Debased databases

At this point, a word of caution about off-the-shelf computer databases. If it takes about a minute to write a name and address, 18,000 of them will take a very long time, even with ready access to a source for all the information. It is such a beguiling proposition to resort to an off-the-peg database from one of the many commercial suppliers. If you decide to do this, make sure that what you are buying (or begging, borrowing or stealing) is targeted accurately enough to help you meet your objectives. If your objective is to communicate, then how will you measure what communication has taken place? Do not be surprised if a massive communication effort produces very poor results. The chances are that the person who received your mailing also receives stuff from all the other organisations who are using the same mailing list, so you will need to be lucky to get a response. The most important thing to ask about the mailing list is: *will my material be delivered to the person in the organisation who can be of most benefit to my network*? If the material is addressed to 'The Chief Executive', or to a named individual who left three years ago then you can draw your own conclusions.

Never trust a computer

I keep a hard copy of all the names and addresses of my contacts, so that if, and when, something goes wrong with the computer I have a reliable back-up. In the early stages, I actually wrote out all the names and addresses on file cards. The initial slog of writing out the cards more than repaid itself, and I am sure that my computer system was no more accident prone than many others which will be used as a matter of course by network managers.

One way or another, you have a list of people whom you think would be interested in your network, so how do you let them know that you are in business? One device which is commonly used is the Launch Event.

A LAUNCH EVENT

If you are setting up a network from scratch, or have decided to relaunch a flagging network (see Chapter 4), then you will need to consider an event to mark the launch. If the network is in its infancy, then there will be few tangible benefits to attract people. These are best considered under the headings of *venue, entertainment* and *refreshments*.

Venue

How many people are you expecting to attend? Will you need extra space to set up an exhibition? How much can you afford to pay? How long will you need the venue for? In addition to the event itself, will you need time to get ready before, and clear up afterwards? Will you need a public address system, overhead projector, screen, chairs, tables, exhibition stands, and, most important of all, a glass of water for the speaker? Do you want the venue itself to be a major attraction? One company used the QEII luxury liner for a one-day conference, which was certainly a big attraction, and it had the added advantage of solving the age-old problem of late arrivals and early departures, as the conference took place while the ship was at sea!

Entertainment

If your launch event is a formal meeting of a network steering group, then you would, of course, provide an agenda, with the anticipated timings of each item. This degree of planning is just as important for launch events which take a different form. You need to state clearly the purpose of the event, and make sure that everything that happens during it reflects that purpose. Any speakers will need to be thoroughly briefed on the whole event and their particular contribution to it. If your budget will allow you to have a famous speaker at your launch event, then make sure that people's recollections of the proceedings consist of rather more than just your guest speaker's name! A useful tip is to write down the three key points that you want your audience to remember after the event.

Imagine their being interviewed by a journalist as they leave: which three things would you like them to tell her? Then concentrate on reinforcing these three aspects so that they are branded on their memories. When you select speakers, be sure that they will find it easy, and comfortable, to be enthusiastic about your chosen issues.

Refreshments

No matter how good your entertainment, passive listening will not give participants any experience of the benefits of belonging to your network. This appreciation of the benefits of belonging can only come from networking, so allow time for this to happen, preferably after the entertainment, so that everyone has a common experience to build on at the beginning, when conversation can be sticky. If one of the three key messages was that something needs to be done by the participants, then a chance to eat and mingle will give the network manager the opportunity to set the action in train.

To summarise, the key to success is to be clear about what you want from the event, and to allow plenty of time to achieve it. Prominent speakers are often booked up months in advance, so if a speaker is your main priority then be flexible with the dates and times that you offer. This may mean that you have to compromise on the choice of venue, but this sort of choice is better acknowledged at the planning stage than a fortnight before the event.

MEDIA COVERAGE

Do you have something important to say? Is it new, and does it matter? If the answers are yes, and you want to get media coverage for your event, then these tips from Emma Sharp, head of public relations at MCI, will be useful:

- Decide which section of the media will be most interested in your network (eg business editor or arts and entertainment editor) so that you can target your material at specific individuals.
- Ring a journalist before you send an important release to 'warm him up' to it. Once you have sent the release, follow it up to make sure it has been received. If the story will not be used, ask why, but do not be over zealous.
- Try to arrange a meeting with the journalist to explain what your network is going to do.
- Case studies are also a very good means of attracting coverage and letting your network bask in some reflected glory.
- If you are inviting journalists to cover an event, ten days' notice is normally sufficient.
- For radio and TV interviews, always get a brief from the journalist and run through the questions.
- Don't speak 'off the record' as this is dangerous, and if you work for an organisation which has a media relations department check with them anything you are thinking of doing.

Press releases

Always send a press release to a named person. Ideally it should be two pages long, with the story in the first paragraph followed by facts in descending order of importance, with quotes at the end. Always feature quotes from the network manager.

All press releases should be dated and have a contact name, address and telephone number. They should be double-spaced with wide margins so that they can be easily sub-edited on the page. If there are two press releases of equal importance, the one that does not have to be retyped is more likely to get published. Every press release should have the purpose of your network summarised in one sentence. Finally, offer photographs to go with your story.

Deadlines

The time of day you contact a journalist can greatly influence how receptive she is to your story. Daily newspapers are busy in the afternoons, evening newspapers are busy in the mornings, and it is better to avoid their busy periods. Sunday papers work a Tuesday to Saturday week, and, like weeklies, are busier in the run up to the day they are printed. It is best to contact Sundays and weeklies on the day after publication.

When dealing with journalists, establish their deadline and get back as quickly as possible, or they will not bother again. Keep a press book to log enquiries with the date, nature of enquiry and deadline. This will help you monitor the nature and number of calls, and help you assess the effectiveness of your public relations effort.

Fail to plan and you plan to fail

Even if you are not going to send anything to a journalist, it is good discipline to write an account of the launch event in the style of a newspaper article, including a headline, right at the beginning of the planning process. This will give you a model with which to compare reality as events unfold, and will give you early warning of deviations from plan. For example, decide at the beginning how many invitations you will send out and when you will expect to receive responses, and if possible estimate how many will be acceptances. You can also make contingency plans for dealing with too many, or too few, acceptances. At a relaunch event I attended, only two of the guests were not on the committee of the organisation. So a great deal of money was spent in running an event to tell a lot of people what they already knew! This was a waste of an opportunity to make contact with those who were unaware of the organisation's existence.

If you draft a press release about your launch event you will soon realise how difficult it is to make your event novel and attractive. Whatever you think of, it has probably been done before, and moreover by someone with a budget far greater than yours! But I hope these ideas will help you manage the process better, while at the same time allowing you to let your imagination roam unfettered.

Here's one I made earlier

You may find it easier to adapt and build on someone else's plan, rather than begin with a blank sheet. In that case you might find this summary of the CILNTEC/MCI

Network launch of assistance. Please remember that it is no more than an example, and it is very unlikely that anyone else would want to stick precisely to this timetable.

December 1991	Started planning launch event.
6 January	Letter from TEC chairman to principal speaker, a professor of management.
23 January	Letter to a leading financial institution to ask whether we could hold the event there.
24 January	Professor agreed to speak on 20 February at lunchtime.
31 January	Briefing of professor (nb find out as much as possible about your speakers, and be prepared for searching questions about your network).
4 February	Invitations received from printer, and food and venue arrangements finalised.
5–7 February	200 invitations posted.
6 February	Brief other main speaker (Andrew Summers, MCI chief executive).
7 February	Press release sent out.
12–13 February	150 publicity packs assembled for distribution to participants at launch.
14 February	MCI publicity material sent out to important potential network members who had declined invitation (one of these attended her first Network event nearly a year after the launch — moral: never give up!).

18–19 February	Produce handouts for launch (agenda, participant list, thanks expressed to those who helped with launch, menu for buffet lunch). With 70 acceptances and 50 refusals, there were 80 telephone calls to be made to try and finalise numbers. Very few acceptances unearthed.
19 February	Brief launch event chairman, including biographies of three speakers. Prepare own speech.
20 February	Launch event, buffet lunch and exhibition of CILNTEC's products. Three speakers who covered: management development in general (professor); MCI's contribution to management development (Andrew Summers); and encouragement to local organisations to work towards management development through participation in the MCI Network (network manager).
21 February	Thank you letters drafted for chairman to send out and write-up of the launch prepared for newsletters etc.
5 March	Pay bills.

If I were to do this again, I would like more time between issuing the invitations and the Launch, so that I could follow up non-responses more effectively. Also I would be more proactive in dealing with the media.

OTHER EVENTS

Events are the proof of the pudding for the network, because they require the participation of more than just the network manager. At the launch event you will probably attract the mildly curious as well as the enthusiastic. Many of them will come to hear your guest speaker, but will never come again. Events are where network members can be persuaded to network by the network manager, who should be determined to ensure that those who come meet whoever they need or want to see. The network manager moves around like a tugboat manoeuvring the big ships into position. This is not to say that network members will not make contact at other times, but it will be more difficult for the network manager to monitor.

As with the launch event, planning is the key. The network manager will have only a limited amount of time and money to spend on each event, so those resources have got to be invested sensibly. Like the launch event, you need to consider venue, entertainment and refreshments, but now you are dealing with a series rather than a one-off. The series needs a logical thread to connect each event, and you may find that you are involved in a number of series running in parallel, with perhaps one series aimed at novices, and the others at old hands. The logistics may become awkward if the novices progress at different rates, but this sort of problem is better addressed at the planning stage, rather than as you go along.

How long will your series last?

This problem arose at an Executive Job Search Network I helped to establish. We ran fortnightly meetings, and tried to look at a different topic at each meeting, which put an increasing burden on the committee. Because we failed to keep records of who came to each session, it took us longer to realise than it should have done that our membership was turning over about every three months. It was therefore more sensible, and less of a burden for the committee, to repeat a three-month cycle rather than seek to provide something new every time.

Keep the exit in sight

If you are trying something for the first time, then make your early plans as flexible as possible, so that if you start with lunchtime meetings, but find no one comes, you can switch to evenings. Remember, you will not be able to please everyone, so aim to cater for your key participants identified during the mailing list preparation stage.

I have found it best to aim for a mixture of formal input and informal mingling so that everyone who comes will know that they will leave the event with increased knowledge, even if they do not increase their network of contacts. And if the formal input precedes the informal mingling, then even someone who is there for the first time will have a common experience to share with the more seasoned members of your network. The first impressions of a network are obviously crucial, but it is easy for the network manager to forget what impression the network will make on the newcomer.

NEWSLETTERS

If you have decided that the size of your network makes it impossible for you to make frequent personal contact with most of your members, then you have to consider other ways of keeping in touch. One of the most popular is to issue a newsletter, but too many of them are appalling rather than appealing. If you send out a scruffy newsletter whose only interest is in its spelling mistakes, then you are doing more harm than good.

Before you write a single editorial, look at the competition. What other promotional material is likely to be jostling yours for attention in the in-trays of your network members? Are they used to glossy brochures which have been designed and produced by professionals? Get as many as you can, and spread them out on a table. Then see what you can do with the resources you have, and if you cannot compete by newsletter then use the resource for something more effective.

If you decide to produce a newsletter, then do not omit the venture from your network objectives. What sort of return are you looking for from your investment?

The first objective for a newsletter will probably be to get it issued regularly, and the desperate scramble for material and the constant battering of deadlines can too easily become totally engrossing to the detriment of any longer term strategy. Once again, I'm afraid it is back to asking what would happen if your newsletter did not go out. (Sorry to dampen your enthusiasm so early — but just who will issue your newsletter when you are ill? And if it doesn't go out, would anyone notice?)

My own newsletter served to advertise the network events, and each issue had a dated booking form in it so that I could tell which issue led to which bookings. This gave regular feedback about the effectiveness of my efforts, and also allowed me to compare this method with others. The circulation eventually reached 700, and I got a response from about ten people a month. I also had a page in the CILNTEC quarterly business magazine, which had a circulation of 18,000, but this had only resulted in half a dozen enquiries from three issues! If bookings had started to drop off, I would have had to look very carefully at the newletter's other two objectives.

The first was to offer something tangible to those who asked, or may have been interested in, what the network actually *did*. I could not respond personally to every request for information, and very often people imagined that they were too busy for me to visit them, but by using the newsletter I could get the basic message across very quickly and, I hoped, attractively.

The other objective of the newsletter was to force me to master the product that I was selling, in order to present it more effectively to others. Retailers like W H Smith have on display in their shops the certificates that their staff have earned for their product knowledge. I was also expected, as network manager, to be knowledgeable about my 'products'.

The network manager needs a sound product knowledge coupled with good communication skills, so that the understanding can be shared with the network member. The product knowledge must stem from the objectives of the network, which is why a regular newsletter is so useful to a network manager. If the newsletter is supporting the objectives of the network, then its contents should be appropriate to those objectives. Whoever compiles the newsletter must be accumulating and storing product knowledge. It is well known that a good way to improve your understanding of a topic is to discuss it with someone else. A regular newsletter is also a voracious consumer of material, and so the editor is constantly increasing the width and depth of his or her knowledge in a search for something fresh to write about. Where possible I suggest that the network manager should play a major part in producing the newsletter, or else all the product knowledge is going to end up in someone else's head.

I found that in the absence of regular courses, the looming newsletter deadline together with a shortage of copy was just the incentive I needed to get to grips with the latest news about management development.

There are other, and possibly cheaper, ways to achieve both these subsidiary objectives, and they should be explored if the newsletter fails to meet its primary objective effectively. A useful way to investigate whether the network manager's perceptions of the newsletter match those of the recipients (we cannot assume they are *readers!*), is to issue a questionnaire once a year. Questionnaire evidence is notoriously difficult to analyse sensibly, but at least the discipline of drafting the questions forces the network manager to step back from the routine preoccupation of editing, to take a more strategic view of the venture.

Does the network newsletter provide a means for the network manager to pass on his understanding of how network members are contributing to the achievement of the network's objectives? You may think you have understood what someone is doing on the basis of a brief conversation during a conference coffee break, but wait till you have to write about it in a newsletter! It is sobering to discover how many of the basic questions — who, why, where, what, when and how — do not get asked. You are also more likely to remember the replies if you know you will have to write about them later.

If you need other ideas about newsletters, turn to Chapter 7 (Further Reading).

OTHER BENEFITS OF NETWORK MEMBERSHIP

In managing a network there is no substitute for regular contact between members, but there may be some resources left over to devote to other benefits of network membership. As with all the other activities described in this chapter, the network manager needs to be sure that the benefit will work hard to further the network's objectives. Other benefits fall into two categories:

'One-off' benefits

There is scope to be experimental with these, and they should only be offered once in case they turn out to be a disaster.

You might launch a competition to generate interest, or fund some research whose results would be exclusive to the network. This would involve designing a research project which would rely on evidence provided by members of the network. If the findings are of wider importance, then publication outside the network can be considered, and here network members are exchanging the right to exclusive access for the less tangible feeling of worth that comes from being a member of a network that produces work of considerable importance to the wider community. This may in turn lead to a higher profile for the network, and maybe increased membership.

Longer term benefits

If you start providing long-term benefits for your network members then you obviously need to be sure of the business case. A professional education scheme; library/study facilities; advisory/information services; an annual conference; a paid secretariat — all of these will cost a great deal of money. There is a danger that raising money for the upkeep of prestigious premises becomes the only objective of the network. Membership numbers may start to decline.

At this point we have returned to the theme with which I began this chapter. All these benefits of network membership may start to attract many new members, or they may signal the beginning of the end. Is the change in membership profile consistent with the network's objectives? Should the network manager be ashen-faced or over the moon?

CHECKLIST

- What are the objectives for your network?
- Are your objectives SMART?
- Who are your top twenty network members?
- What would you expect from a successful launch event?
- How will you improve the media coverage of your network?
- How will your network events help meet your objectives?
- If you issue a newsletter, how does it help you meet your objectives?
- Why do you offer/not offer other membership benefits?

The brainshaker question is:
What is the advantage of using a luxury liner for a launch event?

Networking eases the task of collecting basic information and reduces the risk of depending on blinkered judgements. It allows a body of expertise to be tapped across organisations, which is especially useful in rapidly changing areas such as EU directives and their implementation in different states.

Robin Chater
network coordinator
The EU Employers Network

The most interesting and successful networks are those which do not simply bring together people with a common interest. Diverse networks provide greater energy and more ideas. Common Purpose is based on the premise that a network of people from a wide range of sectors and backgrounds can bring about new approaches and solutions to old problems.

Alison Coburn
London director
Common Purpose

4: How much will it cost? How long will it take?

HOW MUCH WILL IT COST?

This is most easily dealt with under two headings: fixed costs and variable costs.

Fixed costs

As I have been pointing out relentlessly, networks do not manage themselves, they need a manager. If the network is being run in a commercial context, then that manager should have the network management activities reflected in her job description, and Chapter 5 gives examples of the activities that need to be included. From this it should follow that the time required to manage the network will be included in the organisation's budget calculations. This will indicate the amount of fixed costs involved.

The whole job need not be done by one person, and some of the routine tasks of network management can be done by junior people. The important thing to remember is that the network members need to have confidence in the network manager, so it would be a false economy to entrust *all* the functions to someone lower down the hierarchy.

Just as the whole range of network management activities do not need to be done by the same person, so also it need not be a full-time job for one or more people. The typical MCI network manager has one or two days a week to spend on MCI matters, with the balance of their time very often being spent on related activities such as NVQs or Investors in People. Since both these areas are closely related to management development, you could argue that they were part of the network manager's job to the extent that they improved his product knowledge.

Who does what?

However you choose to allocate the workload, it should be clearly allocated, and the implications considered. If the objective is maximum impact and rapid growth, then a full-time manager is required. This was the situation at CILNTEC, where we realised that potential members would quickly lose interest if there was any delay in responding to their initial enquiry. They would also tend to lose interest if there were a network in name only, which never seemed to do anything other than recruit new members.

Can you afford to do without?

If you were expecting to see a price quoted here, as if a network manager were like a new piece of computer software, then I am sorry to disappoint you. Costs are dependent on how many people do it, how long they spend, and how much you pay them. What I have tried to indicate though, is that if you take network management seriously in the commercial context then you should consider your investment carefully, and decide what return you are expecting from it. This means that you will have to calculate your own costs rather than relying on any estimate by me.

Shall we talk shoestrings?

Outside the commercial context, of course, you are less likely to be able to run to a full-time network manager. Nevertheless, it helps to give somebody the title and the responsibility. He should then see that the network management functions are carried out as described in this book, even if some are done by the chairman, secretary or other committee members.

Still outside the commercial context, but in a special category, many unemployed people find themselves managing a network. In this case, the object of the network is to get them back into employment. Time is usually not a problem, although the variable costs described in the next section may be. If you are looking for another job, just seeing yourself as a network manager can help you take a positive and methodical approach. It will help, when reading through the next section, to see how you can adapt the approach to your own particular circumstances. You will also find that Chapter 6 deals specifically with managing a network to find another job.

Variable costs

Having appointed somebody to be the network manager and calculated how much it is going to cost you to employ them, you can then allocate a budget to meet variable costs. As a very rough guide, it may be helpful to know that my budget for the first year of the CILNTEC/MCI Network was £20,000. Most of this paid for the design and printing of the newsletter, and since this was the major marketing device of the network, the expenditure reflected the network objectives.

Juggling expenditure

The net cost of the newsletter could have been brought down by reducing the quality or quantity (fewer printed or fewer issues); or by generating income by charging or selling advertising space. Each of these options should be considered against the network's objectives, but they may indicate that the net cost should be increased, if, for example, important members of the network ask for far more copies of the newsletter.

HOW LONG WILL IT TAKE?

Like a good story, a network should have a beginning, a middle and an end. So the exploration of how long it takes to set up and run a successful network falls naturally into three parts. And then there is a fourth part — the *post mortem*.

The beginning

We looked at the early stages of a network in the previous chapter, and now I want to move on to consider two hazards which may shipwreck you. Representing Scylla is the danger of setting up a network in too great a hurry. In my experience, you must allow a year to establish a network. If you decide to abandon it before the year is over you will not only have wasted all you have spent on launching it, but you will also suffer considerable embarrassment.

Having successfully skirted the threat of Scylla, you must keep a wary eye open for Charybdis, which with networks is the danger of getting stuck in the initial stages of setting up your network. There is a problem that the network manager never escapes from the frontiersman mindset. To guard against this danger I am going to stress once more that a network needs to be *managed* to be effective. So to help we can turn to the basic principles of management. There are many books about management, and there will be something of use to the network manager in almost all of them, though surprisingly the word *network* is very rare in the indices.

Back to basics

As this is a short, practical book, I will confine myself to a very brief look at the essence of management — the management cycle. Appropriately enough I have illustrated it with the penny farthing bicycle in Figure 4.1.

The person atop the penny farthing is the manager, and in order to move forward she has to keep going through the management cycle. If you stop, you come a cropper, so there is a mnemomic to help remember the four activities. It is the memorable word SPAM!

Set objectives

Plan how to meet them

Act

Monitor your progress, and then . . .

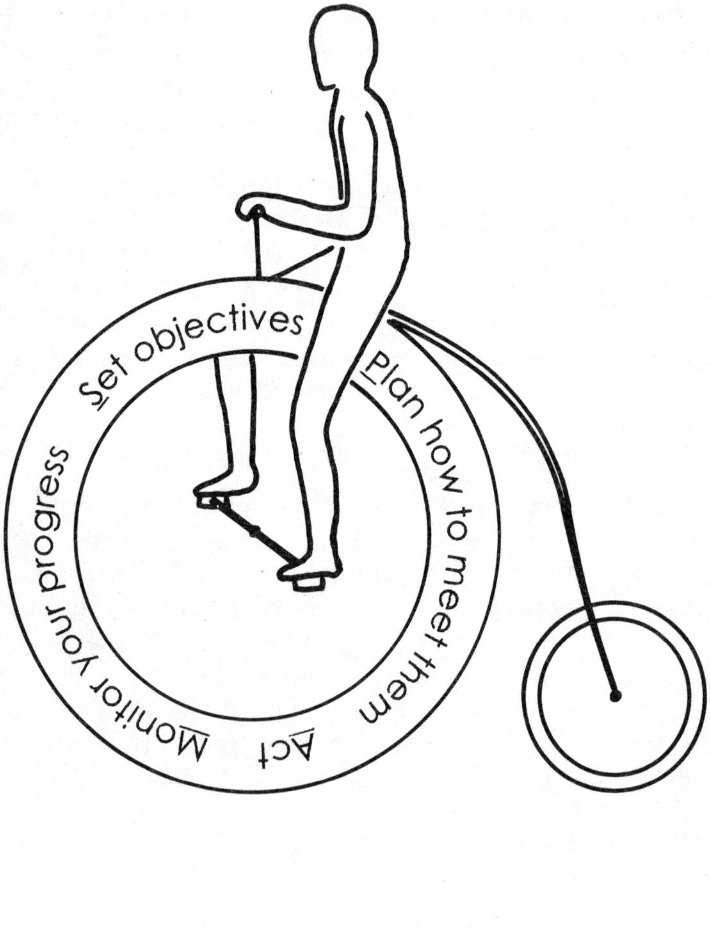

Figure 4.1 The management cycle

Set new objectives

Plan

Act

Monitor, and then . . .

The mnemonic is a useful way to remember the four activities, but you can begin with any of them, you do not have to start at S. Where you choose to start will probably reflect your particular strengths or preferences, and few people excel at all four. That is why I show the management cycle as a penny farthing — unless you keep pedalling, you lose momentum and fall off. It may not be a new approach, but it is certainly revolutionary!

Let us start with setting objectives. You may be setting them yourself, or with others. In either case, you might like to refer back to the section on setting SMART objectives in Chapter 2.

With the CILNTEC/MCI Network, the ideal number of contacts for one person to handle was about 500. The first objective for the network was therefore 500 contacts. With efficient monitoring it was easy enough to see how I was doing. Put simply, with a target of 100 new names on the database each month, it would take five months to reach the 500. Was that rate of progress possible? How likely would it be, for example, that all 100 new names would ask the network manager to visit them? How long would each visit take? How many man/hours would that total? If it seems attainable, then you need not change the objectives, nor the plans that follow from them. If progress is too fast or slow then objectives and consequent plans can be changed.

Table 4.1: CILNTEC/MCI Network manager's activities

October 1991–March 1993

Visits to/from	140
Conferences	40
Training events	40
Management open learning packages reviewed for MCI	7
Network events	10
Newsletters issued	8

Note 1 The Network was started in October 1991, and so network events and the newsletter did not start until well into 1992.
Note 2 The network manager was allowed to spend all his working time on network-related activities.

Pace yourself

Getting the pace right is one of the most difficult parts of managing a network, and if no one is doing the managing there is nothing to prevent the network from going out of control. Returning to the penny farthing, the network needs balance. You can lose balance by going too slowly, or too quickly.

It may help you to judge the correct pace for your network if we compare two networks in their initial stages.

Table 4.1 shows the various activities that went on during the year and a half when I ran the CILNTEC/MCI Network. This network was under pressure to grow quickly because it was one of the ways in which the newly-formed TEC could advertise its presence. The TEC was launched with a fanfare, and tried hard to achieve some results before the notes died away. This meant that the major part of my effort went into attracting new members, rather than cementing relationships between existing members.

In a year I made, or received, visits to or from just over 100 people who wanted to know about the network. Over the same period there were six network events, and some sixty people attended. There were also six issues of a newsletter. If we look at the notional time per member figure, with 700 on the newsletter mailing list, it represents an average of 2½ hours per member per year. That may not seem much, but the Pareto rule applies here, so that 20 per cent of the members take up 80 per cent of the network manager's time.

Prioritise

The art of network management is to ensure that the highest yielding 20 per cent get the 80 per cent of your attention. If you study the methods of professional fundraisers, you will notice that they rank the network members by salary or net worth and then concentrate their efforts on the top 20 per cent.

By way of contrast, compare the average of 2½ hours per year per member of the CILNTEC/MCI Network with the 40 hours per year of the Executive Job Search Network. A committee of six organises a fortnightly meeting for about ten unemployed executives. The meetings each last about two hours, and the planning meetings a further two hours each about every six weeks. The amount of time per network member therefore works out at 40 hours per year. Only experience can show whether an unemployed person is going to require more time than an MCI Network member, but I wonder how many network managers consider this aspect when they set up their networks. A quick look at network objectives will show that it is usually ignored. This may be because the network manager does not want to acknowledge that the amount of resource available is limited. With the CILNTEC/MCI Network there was a budget of £20,000 in year one plus a full-time network manager, whereas with the Executive Job Search Network, the events were organised by volunteers in their spare time with a budget of about £50! In setting objectives you must cut your coat according to your cloth.

Which straw will be the last?

If this aspect were to be considered fully then the network manager would realise that a point can be identified at the planning stage where growth will have gone out of control. The time per member has become so small that the network manager should have worked out how to use the network members to share the workload. At this point, of course, the network reaches maturity — the middle phase, with network members working *together* to achieve a common objective. Until now their relationship has been solely with the network manager, and not with each other.

If we return to the penny farthing analogy, it can be difficult to apply the brakes just as we experience the delicious sensation of speed resulting from our exertions. The fable of the hare and tortoise has something to teach us at this point.

The middle

What should prompt the network manager to start thinking about applying the brakes? It is time to consider consolidation rather than expansion when you can produce a prospectus for your network that contains the following information:

1. History of the network.
2. Who the members are, or, if there are many of them, what kind of people are members.
3. What common interest unites the members.
4. The network's strategic aim.
5. The network's mission statement.
6. Network activities and achievements.
7. Plans for the future.
8. Benefits of network membership.
9. Whom to contact for more information.

In applying the brakes we need to refer to the evidence gathered as a result of monitoring in the early stages. What activity brought in new members most quickly? That is the activity to cut back on, but that may be difficult if it is what you do best. Once more, careful monitoring is essential to ensure that the target number of members is maintained.

In the rapid growth phase of a network, because it is shortlived, there should not be much natural wastage of members unless there is no demand for your product. As the network becomes middle-aged the passing of time will promote natural wastage.

Are your records straight?

There is a danger of the database becoming unreliable as, for example, network members move to other parts of their organisation or to new jobs. If you have records which show when each member joined they can be used to plan check-up contacts. According to circumstances, the network manager can telephone, write to or visit a set number of members each week. This is easier to do, in my experience, if the member is receiving a regular newsletter because you can justifiably ask whether they want to continue to receive it. If the member has moved away, you should try to find a replacement contact. As a result you may end up with two members (one old and one new), or just the new one, or none at all. Again, careful monitoring is necessary so that you get a timely indication of the results of the check-up contacts.

Consolidation

During the maturity phase of the network the number of members ought to remain fairly stable around the level you have set as one of your objectives. Sufficient 'bricks' will be available to build the structure, and the network manager's job now will be to strengthen the bonds, to ensure that the network becomes more close-knit. At this stage the network manager is looking for repeat business rather than new business, so that the objectives need to be set accordingly.

At the rapid growth phase, the emphasis would have been on getting new members, but in the maturity phase the emphasis must shift towards keeping existing members involved, with new members being attracted solely to make good natural wastage, or to improve the balance of the membership.

Planning

Just as we looked at setting objectives in the previous section, we now need to look at planning, the second slice of SPAM. At this stage the network manager should plan to shift the focus of the network's activities from recruiting new members to the cementing of relationships between existing members. This means that the interactions change from being between the network manager and individual members to being between one member and another.

Drawing conclusions

Once the network has reached maturity it may be helpful to try to represent it diagramatically. The object of drawing pictures will be to highlight the areas of strength and weakness in your network. These strengths and weaknesses can remain stubbornly concealed as long as your network is shown only as an alphabetically ordered list of names.

If you find the prospect of drawing a network diagram daunting, then use your networking skills to contact someone who produces local or wide area computer network diagrams. The same principles apply, but you will be illustrating the links between different categories of network member, whereas the computer expert will be showing the links between different kinds of hardware.

Here are some ideas for diagrams:

1. Get a map and stick pins in it to represent each network member. This will quickly show any areas where you are under-represented. Alternatively, you can use a software program which will put a blob on a map by referring to the network member's postcode.
2. A basic line diagram can work quite hard for you if you use plenty of imagination. Different types of network member can be represented by different

symbols, and the frequency of interactions can determine the thickness of the lines which join the symbols. Different types of interactions can be allocated different coloured lines, and the addition of arrows can show who contacts whom. For example, if the network manager sends out a newsletter then all the arrows will point from her to the members, but as soon as a member rings with a query about the newsletter an arrow which points in the opposite direction should be added. As a further refinement, you can use the relative distances between symbols to indicate the frequency of interactions. If you have a large network, the diagram will become unwieldy, so it would be best to concentrate on a section of the network, such as your 20 'key' members.

3. Line diagrams can also be used to show the different relationships that join network members, and perhaps show the network manager which other networks he should consider joining. Figure 4.2 shows that the network manager should consider taking up rugby!

4. Another use of line diagrams can quickly show how many other networks are accessible, and how well your network is bonded. In the early stages the network manager knows each member, but they do not know each other. Each link in Figure 4.3a is a first order link. Figure 4.3b shows second order links, which indicate how you can move from your own network into others via friends, and friends of friends. Figure 4.3c shows how to calculate the density of your network, which is simply the number of actual interactions as a percentage of the number of possible interactions. This figure also shows that the effect on the density of the network of Colonel Mustard's

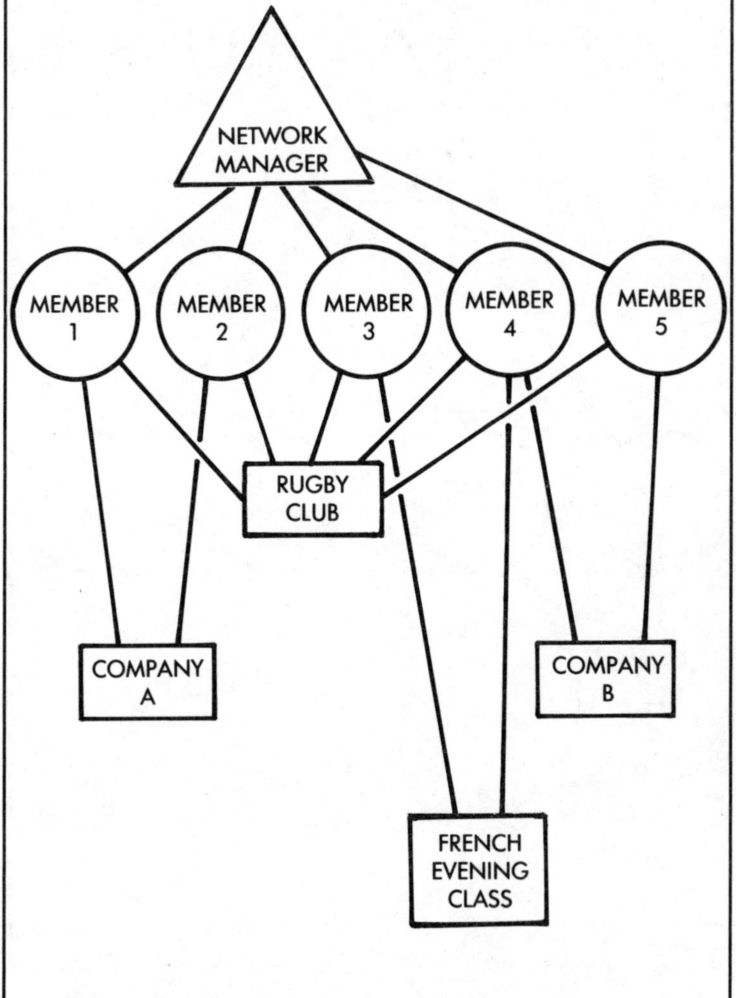

Figure 4.2 Links to other networks

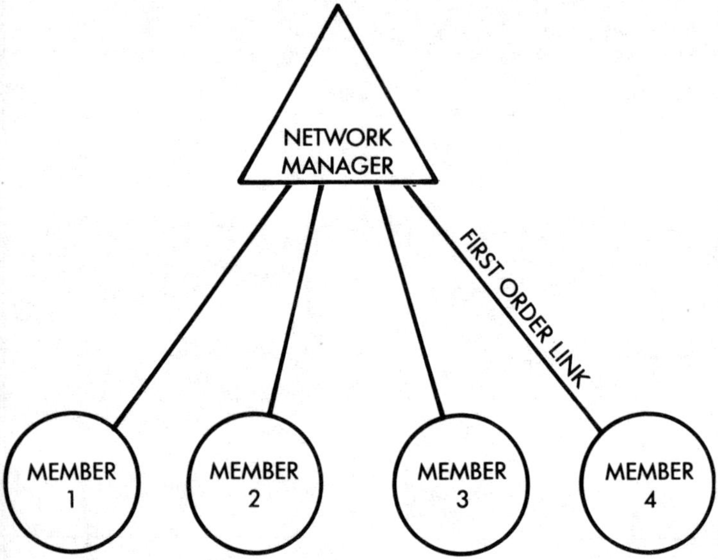

Figure 4.3a First order links

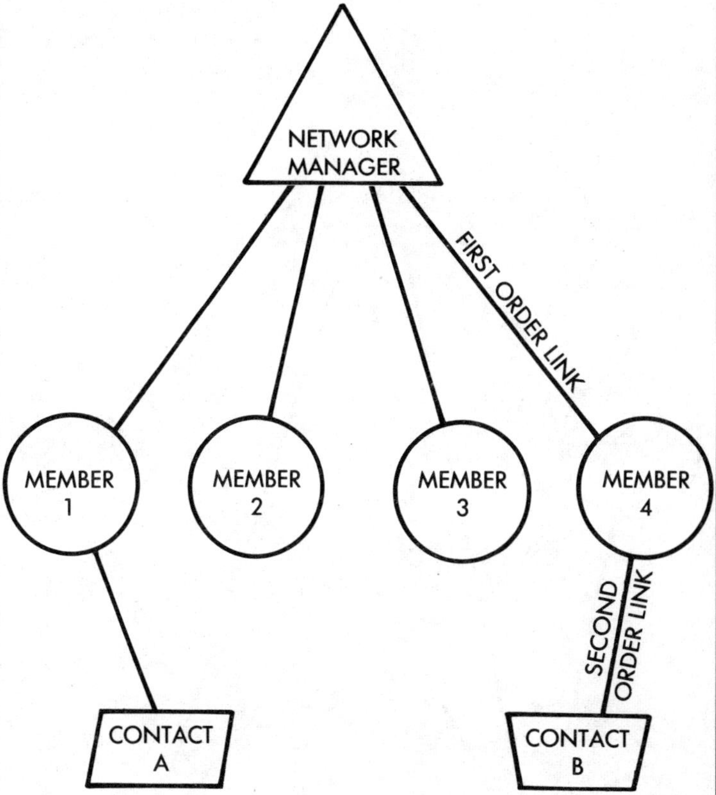

Figure 4.3b Second order links

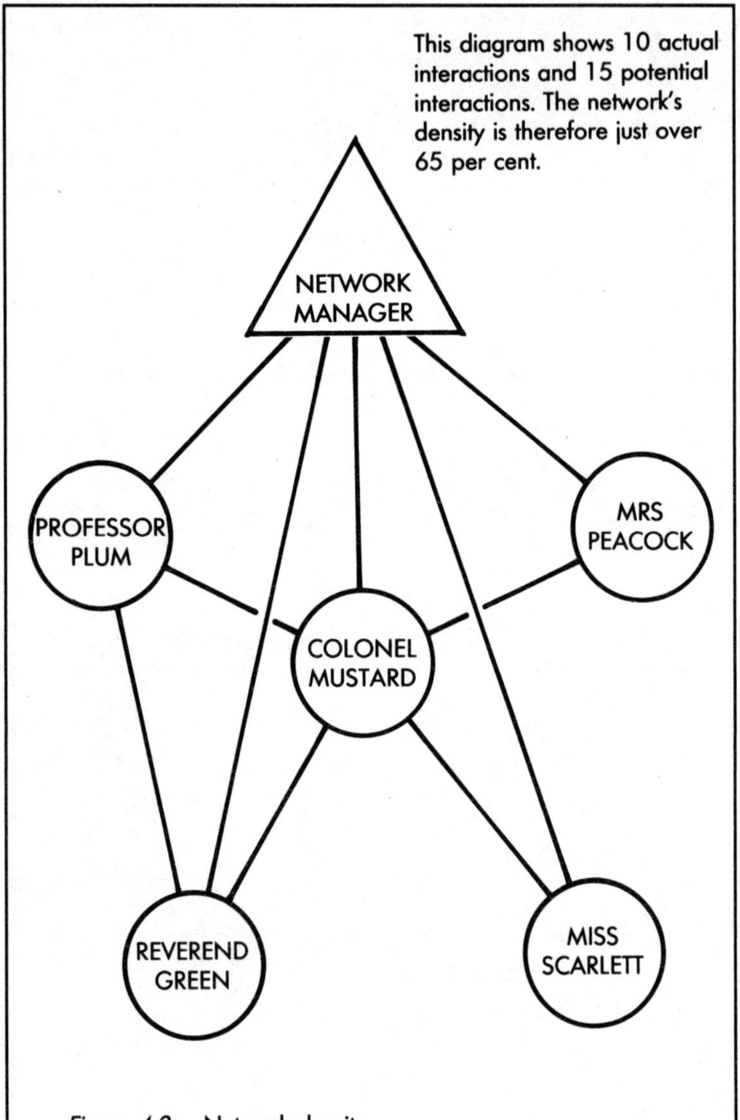
This diagram shows 10 actual interactions and 15 potential interactions. The network's density is therefore just over 65 per cent.
NETWORK MANAGER
PROFESSOR PLUM
MRS PEACOCK
COLONEL MUSTARD
REVEREND GREEN
MISS SCARLETT

Figure 4.3c Network density

removal is far more serious than would be the change to the density if Professor Plum were to disappear.

The end of the network

The end is nigh for many networks, but all too often it is protracted and painful. The problem is usually lack of management — there is no one on the penny farthing to drive the wheels round. The management cycle stops. So what signs will the network pathologist be looking for?

The first place to look is the database. Has *rigor mortis* set in? If we were to contact the members of the network shown on the list, would we use the telephone or a spiritual medium? If nobody knows the status of the database, then that is a worrying sign. One way of checking it frequently is to ask members to give their name, address and telephone number whenever they reserve a place at an event. There is also an annual opportunity to check details if members have to pay a subscription.

Some networks will leave names on their database, despite not having had a response from the person for a considerable time. The names are usually retained because they are prestigious. Such names should be clearly identified and consigned to a dormant category. This category should have objectives set for it like any other category of member. The cost of servicing the dormant category should also be calculated. Is it a luxury you can afford?

Be firm

One way to reduce the size of the dormant category is to make a charge for network services, but even so there may be members who pay up, but play no active part. The network should have a policy for dealing with such members. Keep them because they attract other members, or ask them to leave so that others can have a chance? Choirs that value the quality of their singing carry out regular auditions of existing members, whereas those that value the quality of their social life do not. Another way of dealing with dormant members is the continuing professional development requirement being introduced by a growing number of professional bodies. Attendance at local branch meetings will count towards the number of annual training hours required. At a more humble level, some organisations have emulated the book clubs, and will not renew your membership unless you have attended a minimum number of meetings.

An interesting variation on this theme occurred at the merchant bank County NatWest, which became part of NatWest Markets in 1992. When Alby Cator, the syndications director, arrived at County NatWest he found that poor morale in the company was preventing his team from networking with the other major banks in London. This meant that they were losing their instinctive feel for the market value of various deals that were being put together. The result was that when they tendered for the business they were slightly out of line with the other major firms. They either lost the business or else paid a little more for it than they need have done. The difference between ½ per cent and ⅜ per cent may seem insignificant to most of us, but when you are paying ⅛ per cent more than necessary for ten years on a sum of several millions of pounds then the effect on profits can be disastrous.

Alby Cator's response was to set a networking target for his team that they should get out to meet the other firms in

KNOW YOUR ENEMY

The network saboteur's handbook contains the following rules:

1. Join the network you want to destroy. Death-watch beetles and network saboteurs work much better from within the structure.

2. Criticise the network manager for always arranging events on days you cannot manage.

3. Criticise the network to anyone who will listen.

4. Don't tell anyone in the network your correct address or phone number.

5. Offer help to as many network members as possible — but never deliver.

6. Never pay; never participate; never praise; never part company from the network.

With enough members like you the network is bound to fail!

the market at least twice a week. Their instinctive feel for pricing a deal returned, profitability improved and they won the *International Financial Review* 'Team of the Year' award.

Another place to check when investigating a network's health is to look at the network manager. In many cases, the manager has stamped her authority on the network to such a degree that she *is* the network. We have seen similar examples of charismatic leadership in the company sector, and attempts are now being made to curb the worst excesses that can be perpetrated by a dominant leader who brooks no opposition.

Make them do without you

One network relied on the same secretary for seventeen years. Such devotion to a cause is commendable, but it meant that a fundamental review of the network did not occur until the secretary had to quit. This revealed that a major change of membership had taken place, and a reexamination of the network's objectives had to be carried out. As ever, this is better carried out as part of the regular maintenance procedure, rather than when there is a crisis.

Another secretary wrote in a newsletter that many committee members had completed quite long stints, and would be quite willing to give way to younger members. One way round this familiar problem is to insist that the network manager (and other network 'officials') should make way for someone else after a period of between three and five years. This reduces the risk of domination by the network manager, and may result in a 'retired' network manager or two being available to take over in an emergency. It also introduces an element of succession planning, and who knows, there may even be some training provided for the incoming network manager.

If there is only one person who is willing, or able, to manage the network, then is it worth preserving? What is the network's shared objective, if it relies on one person to carry it out?

Mission impossible?

Having examined the network's database and the manager, the next area to probe is the network's mission statement (or purpose).

Many networks were set up before mission statements became fashionable, and it can be very difficult to establish why the network still functions. An example is the nostalgia association for alumni of a school or college. These were initially set up to promote friendship among past members and to help them keep in contact with Alma Mater. Many used the networking opportunities (and 'ties' is an important component of many!) to further their careers. The only formal contacts with members were written communications and perhaps an annual reunion at a dinner or annual general meeting attended by a small percentage of the total membership. A feature of these associations was that they were usually run by a few dedicated people, and that the commitment of resources from the average member was minimal. There was so little difference between belonging and not belonging, that many regarded it as a cheap insurance policy in case they fell on hard times.

Now though, the members are seen as more than a source of snippets for the newsletter, as the Alma Maters become more ruthlessly businesslike. Members are now seen as a useful source of income, and alumni magazines contain more appeals and adverts, and fewer items about former members, who have suddenly realised that the price of nostalgia has risen sharply. If these networks, which have now become business networks, are not to wither then they need to clarify, and publicise, their mission statements to establish whether they can command the necessary commitment from members. Just what is it that they can do better by acting in concert, than if they acted separately?

Many alumni organisations are now including a compulsory subscription as part of the fees for the student's education, so that everyone is a member, like it or not. But a larger membership is not necessarily a more active, close-knit, or indeed generous, membership. It remains to be seen how many members will value the 'opportunity' to be able to show their appreciation for their education by making a handsome donation to a charitable trust.

Intensive care

Perhaps you are involved in a network that appears to be moribund. I have come across networks that have no more than a box of headed stationery, and not even a membership list. You do not have the well-charted progress through the stages of a network outlined earlier.

Should I repair or terminate? This question confronts us every time a car or washing machine breaks down. With a business network, though, it is more unusual for there to be a clear-cut event, like a breakdown, to force us to confront the issue. That is why I recommended in Chapter 3 that the objectives of the network should be reviewed annually. If there is no network manager, of course, responsibility for the review may not be assigned to anyone, and will never be carried out.

Having decided to carry out a review, however, and search for signs of life, or indeed establish the cause of death, how should you proceed? I will concentrate on a low cost method for structuring a review, on the assumption that readers who are responsible for multi-million pound networks will have access to more sophisticated review procedures.

First, get hold of a small business start-up pack. Many versions are available free from accountancy firms, Training and Enterprise Councils (in Scotland, they are known as Local Enterprise Companies), high street banks or the Department of Trade and Industry.

At first sight many network managers may think that information about starting up a small business is irrelevant, especially if the network has been going for donkey's years. But once you start looking at your network as a *business* then working through the questions posed in small business guides can be a very useful discipline. Typical questions are:

- What is your income likely to be over the next five years?
- What is your expenditure likely to be over the next five years?
- Who are your customers?
- Who are your competitors?
- What are your network's strengths and weaknesses?
- What opportunities and threats await your network?

If you answer as many of these questions as you can, and

face up to the reasons for any 'don't knows', you will have a good idea of your network's chances of survival.

If the chances are low, then the members should be consulted about an orderly liquidation of the network, or perhaps they would support a merger with another network. Now would seem to be a good time to find out whether the members of the network have ever written down any instructions for bringing it to a peaceful end.

A dignified departure

Rather than a picture of one's family on the desk, I recommend a framed copy of the following to act as a *memento mori* for the network manager who considers the network to be immortal:

> 'DISSOLUTION OF THE NETWORK
>
> If at any General Meeting (or equivalent), a majority of the network members feel the network should be ended then a Special General Meeting should be arranged within a month. At that meeting, a further vote should take place, and if there is another majority in favour of dissolution then the network manager should realise the network's assets. If there is any surplus it should be disposed of as agreed at the Special General Meeting.'

Mergers should always be backed up by a sound business case, so that members know what benefits will follow the merger, and when they will materialise. Quite often improved networking opportunities are cited as one of the benefits. When the Institute of Personnel Management

President recommended to his members that they should merge with the Institute of Training and Development, he cited as one of the benefits the improved opportunity for specialist networks to promote learning and develop professional contacts.

If the network can only survive with an injection of extra resources, then you will already have gone a long way towards drawing up the business case to put to members, or other benefactors who may have an interest in keeping the network alive.

If those extra resources will come from you alone, then be particularly careful. Many network members are very enthusiastic about the network, as long as someone else does all the work! If you decide to revive an ailing network, then it is wise to:

- carry out a thorough examination, to see if there is anything worth saving; and
- agree a time limit on your commitment.

CHECKLIST

- What are your network's fixed costs?
- What are your network's variable costs?
- What are your objectives for your network?
- What are your plans for achieving your objectives?
- How will you monitor your actions?
- How will you know when your network should stop growing?

- How will you know when your network should cease?
- Why does your network exist?

The brainshaker question is:
What does a network saboteur have in common with a deathwatch beetle?

When I arrived at Bromley by Bow, in the heart of the East End of London, in 1984, I was confronted by a fragmented local community with a wide variety of groups and individuals with little to connect them. Human existence had become 'privatised', which had many unhealthy consequences for a diverse community struggling to survive in one of Britain's poorest areas. During the last ten years we have provided a 'centre' to connect groups and individuals because we believe that networks of human communities will enrich all our lives.

Rev Andrew Mawson
director
The Bromley by Bow Centre

5: Who should manage a business network?

Most readers will agree that half the population is not as good at networking as the other half. It is only when you ask which half that the friction develops. Rajan and van Eupen have said that 'female employees are seen as being more flexible and adaptable, better at team work, managing change, networking and group support' (Rajan A and van Eupen, P (1989) *Good Practice in the Employment of Women Employees* IMS Report no 183). That use of the phrase 'are seen' worries me, because I cannot tell whether the eyes are male or female. The reference did not sit comfortably in its surroundings either, because it had been dropped into a report which concluded that the reason why many female employees did not reach the top was because of the impenetrable strength of the *male* networks which were determined to preserve the *status quo*.

Enthusiasm is the key

I have seen good and bad network managers from where I sit, on the fence, but there was no correlation with their gender. The crucial difference was belief in their network's objectives. Strong believers want to be good network managers.

Competence

Naturally, disposition and personality play a part in determining who will be excellent network managers, but in this chapter I want to set out what you need to do to be a *competent* network manager. The aim of this book is to help network managers to do their jobs competently. In the unlikely event that competence becomes universal, then we can think about setting up the Chartered Institute of Network Managers to raise standards above the competent level.

MANAGEMENT STANDARDS

There are two elements to the job: one is the *managing* part, and the other is the *network* part. I am going to start with the first element, where someone else, the Management Charter Initiative (MCI), has already done the work for us and produced three sets of management standards — one each for supervisors, first-line, and middle managers. Senior management standards are also being developed.

If this is the first time you have come across these management standards then the easiest way to understand them is this. Imagine MCI has identified a first-line manager that they consider to be competent. They then observe our hero(ine) going about their daily management tasks, and produce a written description of what they do. Rather than describe the activities as they happen, they have been classified into four groups to make them easier to understand. The first group of activities relates to how the manager manages the operations of the organisation. The second group concerns the management of finance; the third, people; and the fourth, information. Each of these four roles of the manager is then divided and subdivided into a number of layers of detail. At the final level of detail, we are given a set of performance criteria, which is what you would have seen the manager doing if you had been the observer.

Let's look at the example shown in Figure 5.1. If we take the role of managing operations, then that can be split into two functions:

1. Maintain and improve service and product operations;
2. Contribute to the implementation of changes in services, products and systems.

These two functions can in turn be split, and the first one has been divided into:

- a Maintain operations to meet quality standards;
- b Create and maintain the necessary conditions for productive work.

Each of these has a list of tasks, all of which must be done if the job is to be managed competently. For the first one

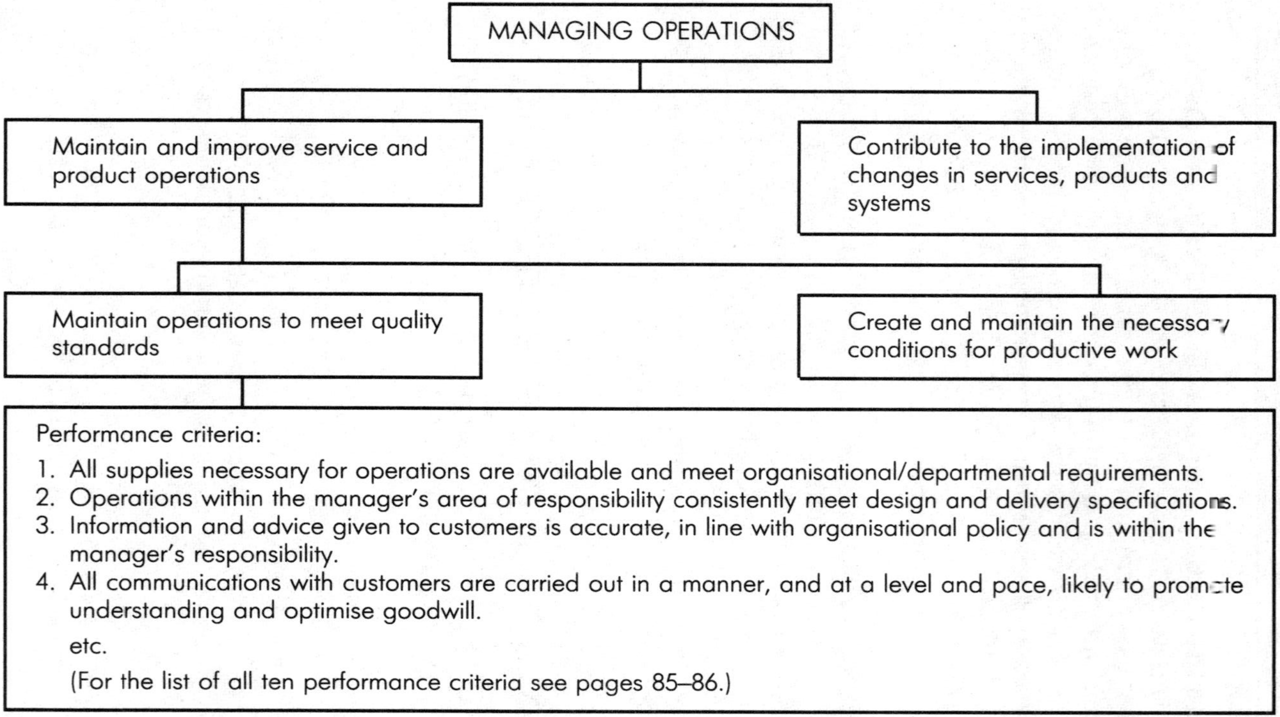
MANAGING OPERATIONS
Maintain and improve service and product operations
Contribute to the implementation of changes in services, products and systems
Maintain operations to meet quality standards
Create and maintain the necessary conditions for productive work
Performance criteria:
1. All supplies necessary for operations are available and meet organisational/departmental requirements.
2. Operations within the manager's area of responsibility consistently meet design and delivery specifications.
3. Information and advice given to customers is accurate, in line with organisational policy and is within the manager's responsibility.
4. All communications with customers are carried out in a manner, and at a level and pace, likely to promote understanding and optimise goodwill.
etc.
(For the list of all ten performance criteria see pages 85–86.)

Figure 5.1 **Structure of the management standards**

we can see that there are ten things to be done, and they are called *performance criteria*. At first sight the list is intimidating, and I found it helpful to apply the performance criteria to a homely and simple task like making a cup of tea, before applying them to the more complex tasks that I carry out at work. If you all have your kettles filled, here is the list:

1. All supplies necessary for operations are available and meet organisational/departmental requirements. (For the job of making a pot of tea, this simply means, have you got the right tea bags? For the more complex job of managing a network the list will, of course, be much longer, but the principle is no different.)

2. Operations within the manager's area of responsibility consistently meet design and delivery specifications. (Whether you are sticking with the tea-making example, or the network management job, I am sure you can think easily of how operations should fit in with this stricture. The same goes for all the rest of the performance criteria.)

3. Information and advice given to customers is accurate, in line with organisational policy and is within the manager's responsibility.

4. All communications with customers are carried out in a manner, and at a level and pace, likely to promote understanding and optimise goodwill.

5. Information about operations which may affect customers is passed to the appropriate people.

6. Systems to monitor quantity, quality, cost and time

specifications for service/product delivery are fully and correctly implemented and maintained.

7. Factors which may cause operations to be disrupted are noted and appropriate measures taken to minimise their effects.
8. Corrective actions are implemented without delay and appropriate staff and customers informed of any changes which affect them.
9. Records related to the design and delivery of operations for the manager's area of responsibility are complete, accurate and comply with organisational procedures.
10. Recommendations for improving the efficiency of operations are passed on to the appropriate people with minimum delay.

Using these basic building blocks, MCI have produced a complete picture of what a competent manager does. And when I say complete I mean, at the most detailed level of performance criteria, 163 different things on the manager's checklist, covering all four roles of management. Depending on what sort of management job is being done, and at what level, it is now possible to select the appropriate performance criteria from the checklist. These in turn can form the basis of a job description, and I am very grateful to MCI and the Department of Employment for letting me quote from the *Management Standards*. If you want further information about these Standards, you will find MCI's address in Chapter 7.

In the case of a network manager, Bryan Fowler of MCI suggests the following activities from the First-line Management Standards:

Contribute to the evaluation of proposed changes to services, products and systems

1. Feedback from subordinates, customers and users is assessed and passed on together with a reasoned evaluation to the appropriate people.
2. Proposals for improvements are passed to the appropriate people with minimum delay.
3. The advantages and disadvantages of introducing changes are assessed against current operational standards and information forwarded to the appropriate people.

Implement and evaluate changes to services, products and systems

1. Relevant details of implementation plans are communicated in a manner, and at a level and pace, appropriate to those concerned and within agreed time scales.
2. Changes in services, products and systems are monitored in accordance with implementation plans and agreed specifications.
3. Outcomes of changes are evaluated against expectations and previous service/production records.
4. Implementation is suitably modified to resolve any problems arising.

Obtain and evaluate information to aid decision making

1. Information is sought and updated on all relevant factors and problems which affect the manager's area of responsibility.

2. Information collected is relevant and sufficient.
3. A variety of sources of information are regularly reviewed for usefulness, reliability and cost.
4. Channels and sources of information are used effectively.
5. Opportunities are taken to establish and maintain contacts with those who may provide useful information.
6. Where information is unclear or difficult to understand, clarification and assistance is sought.
7. Where available information is inadequate, additional information is obtained.
8. Information is assessed for its validity and reliability.
9. Information is organised into a suitable form to aid decision-making.
10. Conclusions drawn from relevant information are based on reasoned argument and appropriate evidence.

Record and store information

1. Information recorded is accurate, complete and legible.
2. Information is recorded and stored using accepted formats, systems and procedures.
3. Information can be retrieved promptly when required.

4. New methods of recording and storing information are suggested/introduced as needed.

Lead meetings and group discussions to solve problems and make decisions

1. A suitable number of people appropriate to the context and purpose of the meeting are invited and attend.
2. The purpose of the meeting is clearly established with other group members at the outset.
3. Information and summaries are presented clearly, at an appropriate time.
4. Style of leadership helps group members to contribute fully.
5. Unhelpful arguments and digressions are effectively discouraged.
6. Any decisions taken fall within the group's authority.
7. Decisions are recorded accurately and passed on as necessary to the appropriate people.

Contribute to discussions to solve problems and make decisions

1. Preparation is sufficient to make a useful contribution to the discussion.
2. The manager's contributions are presented clearly, accurately and at an appropriate time.

3. The manager's contributions are directed at clarifying problems and identifying and assessing solutions.
4. Contributions from, and viewpoints of, others are acknowledged and discussed constructively.
5. Any appropriate departments/team views are represented effectively.

Advise and inform others

1. Advice and information to aid and assist others is offered and disseminated at an appropriate time and place.
2. Information given is current, relevant and accurate.
3. Information is presented in a manner, and at a level and pace, appropriate to the receiver.
4. Advice is consistent with organisational policy and cost and resource constraints.
5. Advice is supported, as appropriate, by reasoned argument and evidence.

As the network manager, this last activity will be one of the most important. Having heard about your network, people will approach you for advice and that first exchange will be vitally important. If the advice you give is current, relevant and accurate and is presented in a manner, and at a level and pace appropriate to the receiver, then you will probably have a satisfied customer who will come back, and also recommend you to others. On the other hand, if you fail to advise and inform others competently you will undoubtedly have a disgruntled customer who will tell many others about their unfortunate experience.

CUSTOMER SERVICE STANDARDS

From this it is clear that network management has a lot to do with customer care. Fortunately, the Customer Service Lead Body has done for customer care what MCI has done for management, and there is now an NVQ at level 3 in Customer Service.

The key purpose for the person responsible for customer service (ie the network manager) is defined as 'To deliver continuous improvement in service to achieve customer satisfaction'. It is vital to apply this to the network manager's task, particularly if the network is an old one and the network manager has been doing the job for a long time. It is only continuous improvement in the service to the network members that will keep the network flourishing.

The way to achieve this continuous improvement has been analysed along the same lines as MCI used to classify management tasks. There are five units, which are divided into 16 elements, and they are further subdivided into 88 performance criteria. Since all these performance criteria are vital for the network manager, I recommend getting the list from the Customer Service Lead Body (see Chapter 7 for address). There is a degree of overlap between the Management Standards and the Customer Service Standards, so the latter are not fully listed, but only those which differ from the Management Standards already listed. These National Standards were developed and produced by the Customer Service Lead Body and the Department of Employment, and I am very grateful to them for giving permission to reproduce some of their performance criteria. Obviously I am not allowed to change any of the words because that would conflict with the concept of their being 'national standards', but if it makes it a little easier, you might consider substituting the words 'network member(s)' for 'customer' throughout.

Organise own work pattern to respond to the needs of customers

1. Advice is sought when limits of own authority and competence are recognised.
2. Practical help is sought assertively to maintain service to customers during peaks in own workload.
3. Practical help is offered to colleagues to maintain service to customers during their workload peaks.
4. Delays are avoided through unprompted extra efforts.
5. Positive responses are made to meet abnormal and unexpected workloads.
6. Plans are made to meet the known demands of future workloads.
7. Contribution of own ideas and experience responds to team and customer needs.

Make use of networks

1. Effective working relationships with other colleagues are maintained.
2. Current organisational networks for monitoring progress are regularly evaluated.

3. Communications with relevant outside parties are effectively maintained on behalf of customers.
4. New contacts likely to benefit customer service are identified through routine scanning of relevant information.
5. Networks are actively used to evaluate new ideas.

Respond to the needs and feelings expressed by the customers

1. Customers' needs are identified promptly and clearly.
2. Customers' feelings are accurately gauged through observation of their behaviour, tone and through sensitive questioning.
3. Customers' needs are identified through sensitive questioning.
4. Own behaviour is always adapted to the perceived needs and feelings of the customer.
5. Perceptions of customers' needs and feelings are regularly checked with customers.

Present positive personal image to customers

1. Treatment of customers is always courteous and helpful even when under stress.
2. Standards for appearance and behaviour are consistently maintained.
3. Equipment and supplies used in transactions with customers are available, up-to-date and in good order.

4. Customers are advised of appropriate statutory measures in operation to protect their health and safety.
5. Opportunities for improving working relationships with customers are actively sought.

Balance the needs of customers and own organisation

1. Persistent attempts to meet customers' needs are made within own limits of authority.
2. Options for mutual gain are identified and communicated clearly to all relevant parties.
3. Options for mutual gain are cost effective for both parties.
4. Organisational limitations are explained clearly to the customers.
5. All possible actions are taken to minimise conflict between customers' needs and organisational limitations.
6. Flexibility in organisational limitations is thoroughly explored and clear policy guidance obtained.
7. Outcomes of proposals put to customers are clearly recorded and stored in the appropriate place.

Identify and interpret problems affecting customers

1. Customers' perceptions of problems are accurately identified and acknowledged.
2. All potential information relevant to the customers' problems is gathered and systematically analysed and prioritised.

3. Customers' problems are clearly summarised using perceptions and information gained from them.
4. Responses are designed to protect customers from unnecessary worry.

Generate solutions on behalf of customers

1. All relevant complaints procedures are examined for solutions to customers' problems.
2. Advice is sought from all relevant sources for solutions to customers' problems.
3. Current procedures are interpreted to generate solutions for customers.
4. Alternative solutions are identified for the customer.
5. Potential new procedures are identified and explored with appropriate colleagues.

Take action to deliver solutions

1. Procedures are promptly activated to solve customers' problems.
2. Clear information about recurring problems or complaints is passed to targeted individuals.
3. Clear information about effective solutions is passed to targeted individuals.
4. Delivery is monitored and suitably modified to resolve any problems arising.
5. Appropriate media are used in all communications with customers.
6. Alternative solutions are presented to the customers.

7. Accurate advice is given to customers of relevant alternative sources of assistance.

Communicate patterns and trends in customers' service within the organisation

1. Measures of customer service are clearly presented in the appropriate form and are based on accurate information.
2. Evaluation of present customer service is measured against current patterns and trends provided by the organisation.
3. Predictions are made about customers' requirements based on the accurate interpretation of patterns and trends.
4. Concise information which accurately illustrates patterns and trends is passed to appropriately targeted individuals.
5. Evaluation takes full account of existing organisational criteria for customers' service.

SUMMARY OF THE JOB DESCRIPTION

We have now explored what the network manager does, and in the preceding sections I have given considerable detail of what competences the network manager needs to acquire and demonstrate. Taking all the details covered, we can boil them down to the two functions of *managing* the network; and *accumulating and sharing knowledge* about the preoccupations of the network members.

PERSONNEL SPECIFICATION

With the job description in mind, we can draw up a personnel specification for a network manager. If we wanted to recruit one, what would we look for?

Physical characteristics

These depend on the type of network, but good health is a requirement for most network managers because they are expected to be able to respond without delay to network members' queries. Prolonged periods of sick leave would inevitably lead to delays. In the absence of good health, then maybe the network manager's job should be shared.

Attainments

These should be sufficient to inspire confidence in the network members. As we noted in Chapter 2, fewer network managers will be able to rely on their position in the hierarchy to command respect because network members will not be part of that hierarchy. In the early stages of a network, the network manager will have to rely on attainments to establish credibility because it takes time to build up the power which comes from being the network manager. This power has to be conferred by network members.

Intelligence

Intelligence levels must be consistent with the product knowledge required and the intelligence of the network members. At the same time, the network manager's intelligence should not be intimidating. On the whole, network members approach the network manager to have their doubts resolved rather than have their lack of knowledge pilloried.

Aptitude

The network manager must have an aptitude to manage! Authority and initiative are required or else the network will not take off, but it is often unclear who, if anyone, has conferred the power on the network manager. The other essential aptitudes are those of enjoying communicating and wanting to change things.

Interests

The network manager's interests should include the objectives of the network. As I said at the beginning of this chapter, what separates the good network manager from the bad one is enthusiasm for the network's objectives. That enthusiasm has to be strong enough to be infectious if the network is to grow.

Disposition

The network manager needs a friendly and cheerful disposition because first impressions are so important for many networks. Whether or not somebody joins a network will often depend on their first meeting with the network manager.

Circumstances

Time available is the most important element here, because the amount of time the network manager can devote to the task will determine the expansion rate and ideal size of the network.

These are all factors which must be considered when

appointing, or applying for a job as, a network manager. A further refinement would be to divide the requirements into essential and desirable, and perhaps list some contra indicators to help decide on borderline cases.

Qualifications

We do not yet have all the panoply of a professional body to look after the interests of network managers, so we cannot short-cut the selection process by asking for the appropriate qualification. However, it is possible to achieve parts of the Scottish/National Vocational Qualifications in Management and Customer Service if you can demonstrate your competence in the aspects of the job shown at the beginning of this chapter. If the whole business of Scottish/National Vocational Qualifications is a closed book, then the best book to open is Shirley Fletcher's which is described more fully in Chapter Seven.

CHECKLIST

- Which of your management competences do you most need to improve?
- Which of your customer service competences do you most need to improve?
- What would you look for if you wanted to recruit a network manager?

The brainshaker question is:
How can the Management Standards help you make a better cup of tea?

The University's Business School finds the opportunities provided by networking of great benefit. Networking allows us to exchange views about management education, training, research and consultancy; and to identify how best we can serve the needs of organisations and individuals in our region.

Jean Fawcett
Dean of Business School
University of North London

From the point of view of REACH, a charity concerned with finding retired (or redundant) professional and business volunteers for other charities, the advantage of networking its pre-retirement course service is that it can tap a wide range of experienced volunteers as speakers. This gives a complete national coverage geographically and allows those attending such courses to put their questions and comments to people who have actually been through the process successfully.

David Barnett
Volunteer development manager
Retired Executives Action Clearing-House

6: Networking into a new job

THE BENEFITS OF NETWORKING FOR JOB SEARCHERS

Contrasting views

I heard this at an Executive Job Search Network meeting: 'This network business is useless: I rang six of my friends in the construction industry, and not one of them could offer me a job!'

However, a survey of nearly 600 managers by Coutts Career Consultants indicated that networking was found to be the best route back to employment for about a third of the redundant managers, while Drake Beam Morin found that half of their clients who got back into work did so through networking.

These orders of magnitude were confirmed by Mike Fogden, chief executive of the Employment Service, the agency which runs government Jobcentres. He said that between 40 and 45 per cent of jobs are filled by informal contact.

Robert Chope, director of the Careers and Personal Development Institute in San Francisco, advises redundant executives to network relentlessly, and to miss no opportunity to tell everyone they meet — even the person on the supermarket checkout and the bank cashier — what sort of job they are looking for.

These views show the importance of attitude. Searching for a job is a job in itself — one of the most important we will ever do. Anybody who is redundant has the enormous advantage of being able to devote the whole working day to the business of job hunting, and as you will have seen from earlier chapters, managing a network requires far more than half-a-dozen telephone calls.

Adapt and thrive

You can take all the ideas in this book about managing a business network and adapt them to your own circumstances. And the best place to start is with the management cycle in Chapter 3. Setting your objective seems deceptively simple — it is obviously to get another job, but if you read the chapter you will see that objectives need to be SMART. Be specific about the type of job you want. This will demand considerable thought, which is why job hunting is described as a job in itself, but remember that the type of job you decide to go for will determine the type of network that you set up. If you stick with your existing occupation, then you will need a network of people who will be familiar with your professional qualifications and track record. On the other hand, you may decide that your speciality has no future, or that you want to seize the opportunity offered by redundancy to switch to something different. Either way, you are going to need a network to give you the basic information about your new career, and provide introductions to influential people.

As you build up and maintain your network of contacts to help you in your search for a new job, you will be developing the competences just described in Chapter 5. You may find that having an NVQ in management or customer service would be a useful addition to your CV, so contact your local Training and Enterprise Council or Local Enterprise Company to see whether they offer one of the schemes which enables unemployed people to work towards an NVQ as part of their job search activities. Some of the TECs and LECs can also put you in touch with a local self-help group for people looking for a new job. Joining such a group is an ideal way to start building up your own network.

But I don't know any orthodontists!

Probably not, but your plumber or bank manager might! Try drawing a personal network diagram and see how you can bridge the gaps between your existing network and those networks which include people from your chosen area. Then get yourself across those bridges by asking people on the other side for advice and guidance. Only when you are safely across should you think about asking for a job, and if you have done your networking thoroughly you should find that employers are approaching you. And don't forget to monitor progress — which assumes that you have time-limited your job search; which in turn assumes that you have identified a starting point. The professional approach will once more be enormously helpful, and you should scale down the plan in Chapter 3 for a network launch event.

Do your homework!

Writers like Peter Drucker (*Post Capitalist Society*, Butterworth Heinemann, 1993) and Charles Handy (*The Empty Raincoat*, Hutchinson, 1994) have suggested that we are moving out of the capitalist era and into one in which the most vital factor of production will be knowledge. And if you want to make money by using your knowledge you no longer need to go to a central location like a factory or office. If you have access to a good communications network you might just as well work from home. It is now much easier, and socially acceptable, to work from home, and many redundant managers are staying there to get back into employment.

CREATING A PORTFOLIO OF JOBS

Rather than work for a single employer, people are building up a portfolio of part-time jobs with the aim of matching the pay and benefits that could be obtained from a traditional job. AZTEC, the Kingston-upon-Thames Training and Enterprise Council is piloting a scheme which pays up to £75 a week for 20 weeks to allow people to build up a portfolio of part-time jobs.

It is likely that portfolio working will increase in popularity. About a million people in the UK currently have more than one job, but this figure may grow quickly. By the year 2000, nearly one and a quarter million jobs, mostly full-time, are expected to disappear from the manufacturing and utilities sectors; but nearly two million jobs in the service sector are expected to be created. More than half of these new jobs, though, will be part-time. (*1990s: Where Will The New Jobs Be?* Institute of Careers

Guidance and Centre for Research in Employment and Technology in Europe, 1992)

Once you switch from a time-orientated approach to a task-orientated approach, everything becomes easier to understand, including how much time the nine-to-fiver spends on non-task activities. Although your productivity should increase in the short term, over a longer period you may suffer from lack of contact with your work colleagues. This is why the network is a vital part of your new work routine, because it compensates for the lack of social interaction that goes on at the traditional workplace. Any organisation that turns to flexible working should use some of the cost savings to ensure that its networks are properly managed, or else they will find it impossible to achieve the benefits that come from teamwork when groups work at the same location.

CHECKLIST

- How will networking help you find a new job?
- How will you adapt the ideas in this book to help you plan your own jobsearch network?
- Are the objectives of your jobsearch network SMART?
- How would you change from conventional work to a portfolio of part-time jobs, of which some would be done at home?

The brainshaker question is: **How do you attract orthodontists into your jobsearch network?**

7: Further reading

They that weave networks shall be confounded

Isaiah 19.9

As I showed in Chapter 1, the word 'network' is not easy to define, and several disciplines have tried to customise it. Sometimes, by reading about the way others approach networking, I have made some useful discoveries. But you need to persevere if you are venturing into a discipline which is unfamiliar. The barrier for the non-expert is that each discipline develops its own jargon, and then uses that jargon to define 'network'. You may need an interpreter, so use your networking skills to find one!

Anthropology, psychology and sociology

Elizabeth Bott wrote an influential study of networks, *Family and Social Network* (Tavistock Publications, London, 1971). She put forward the hypothesis that the members of a close-knit network reach consensus on norms, and exert consistent informal pressure to conform to the norms, to keep in touch, and, if need be, to help one another. As her study involved only a small number of London families, she lacked the data to push her hypothesis further. There is nevertheless a lesson for the network manager who needs to decide whether the network should be exerting consistent informal pressure. If that is an objective, how will the network manager ensure that the network becomes close-knit?

There are a couple of other anthropology books which show how social scientists have grappled with the problem of trying to depict networks in diagrams. They are: J Clyde Mitchell's *Social Networks in Urban Situations: Analyses of Personal Relationships in Central African Towns* (Manchester University Press, 1969); and the *Handbook of Social and Cultural Anthropology* edited by John Honigman (Rand McNally, Chicago, 1973).

Biography

Having a good network of contacts does not guarantee success, but many successful people have used their networks to good effect. Biographies of Armand Hammer, Dr Johnson and Adnan Khashoggi deal with networking on the grand scale.

James Boswell's *The Life of Samuel Johnson* (Edited by John Canning, Methuen, 1991).

Armand Hammer and Neil Lyndon's *Hammer: Witness to History* (Simon & Schuster, 1987).

Ronald Kessler's *Khashoggi: The Story of the World's Richest Man* (Bantam Press, 1987).

Career advancement networks

Is Your 'Net' Working by Anne Boe and Bettie B Youngs

(John Wiley, 1989). The authors predict that networking will be added to the syllabus in business schools.

Paul F Buller and John R Cragun's article 'Networking: The Overlooked Benefit Of Training' in *Training and Development*, volume 45, number 7, July 1991.

Charlene M Solomon's article 'Networks Empower Employees' in *Personnel Journal*, volume 70, number 10, October 1991.

Frank K Sonnenberg's article 'The Professional (and Personal) Profits of Networking' in *Training and Development Journal*, September 1990.

In-company networks

Ram Charan's article 'How Networks Reshape Organisations — For Results' in *Harvard Business Review*, September–October 1991.

Nancy Foy's *The Yin and Yang of Organisations* (Grant McIntyre, 1980). Nancy Foy sets out nine 'laws' for networks, all based on the belief that informality is the key to success. The eighth 'law', for example, is that a network needs a phone number rather than a building. This is good advice for a small network which has just started up, but there are many networks that need a phone number as well as a building, and there is no question of being able to choose.

Management books

On the whole, management gurus do not devote much space in their books to networks as a separate topic. This may be because they depend on their own networking skills for their livelihood, and so they do not want to pass on their trade secrets. As I have shown in this book, though, there is nothing mysterious about managing a network, although you will be a better network manager if you have the right aptitude. See Chapter 5.

Scottish/National Vocational Qualifications (S/NVQs)

Chapter 5 uses the competences from two S/NVQs to show what a competent network manager should be doing. For more details about Customer Services Standards you should contact:

The Secretariat
Customer Service Lead Body
c/o Royal Mail
132 Newport Road
Stafford
ST16 1AA
Tel 0785 226328

and for more details about the Management Standards you should contact:

Management Charter Initiative
Russell Square House
10–12 Russell Square
London
WC1 5BZ
Tel 071 872 9000

If you want to explore NVQs in greater depth, read *NVQs, Standards and Competence* by Shirley Fletcher (Kogan Page, London, 1991). Her book is arranged in three parts. Part 1 is a guide through the intricacies of NVQs. It answers questions that occur to the novice. What exactly are NVQs? What is meant by competence? What is assessment? What makes the new standards different?

Part 2 is for those who are going to introduce NVQs and competence-based standards into their organisation. Shirley Fletcher describes the twelve steps to take, from identifying the occupational areas represented in your business and choosing a pilot area (eg the job of network manager); right up to Stage 12, which means moving on from the pilot to tackle the other occupational areas.

Part 3 has reference material for those who are already familiar with Parts 1 and 2. There are details of all the industry lead bodies from Accounting to Wool, via Chimney Sweeps, Envelope Makers and Thatching.

Part-time working

Patricia Hewitt's *About Time — The revolution in work and family life* (IPPR/Rivers Oram Press, 1993) argues that part-timers should be given the same rights and pay, pro rata, as full-timers. It ought to be possible, by using one's network of contacts, to build up a portfolio of part-time jobs which would yield the same pay and benefits as a single full-time job. Patricia Hewitt shows that some of the best employers are moving towards making it possible, but a lot more needs to be done.

Process re-engineering

Thomas Davenport's *Process Innovation* (HBS Press/McGraw Hill, 1993).

Michael Hammer and James Champy's *Re-engineering the Corporation* (Nicholas Brealey, 1993).

Henry J Johansson's *Business Process Re-engineering* (John Wiley, 1993).

Daniel Morris and Joel Brandon's *Re-engineering Your Business* (McGraw-Hill, 1993).

Publicity

Peter Bartram's *How to write a press release* (How To Books Ltd, 1993).

Dale Carnegie's *How to win friends and influence people* (Cedar Books, 1986).

Graham Jones's *How to publish a newsletter* (How To Books Ltd, 1992).

Richard Nelson Bolles' *What Colour is Your Parachute?* (Ten Speed Press, Berkeley) is an annual publication which is fun to read and full of useful information.

Redundancy

Parting Company — How to Survive the Loss of a Job from Drake Beam Morin, 5 Arlington Street, London, SW1A 1RA.

Tim Heald's *Networks: Who We Know and How We Use Them* (Hodder and Stoughton, 1983). Contains some advice for turning a potential network into a functioning network, if redundancy should strike.

Selling

Peter Clothier's book *Multi-Level Marketing: A Practical Guide to Successful Network Selling* (Kogan Page, London, 1992) describes how to build up a multi-level marketing network. The network consists of people who sell consumer goods to private individuals, in their home or workplace, through transactions initiated and concluded by the salesperson. The network manager's efforts in building up a network of distributors will be rewarded by discounts, bonuses, royalties and other incentives linked to the sales generated by distributors in the network.

Women's networks

Anja Berkelaar's article 'Dutch Women's Networks — A Plea for a Network of Networks' is in *Women in Management Review and Abstracts*, volume 6, number 6, 1991.

Judith Chaney's *Social Networks and Job Information: the situation of women who return to work* (Equal Opportunities Commission, 1981).

Nancy Paul's 'Networking: Women's Key to Success' in *Women in Management Review*, volume 1, number 3, Autumn 1985.

Lily M Segerman-Peck's *Networking and Mentoring: A Woman's Guide* (Piatkus, 1991).

Leonie V Still and Cecily Guerin's article 'Networking Practices of Men and Women Managers Compared' in *Women in Management Review*, volume 2, number 2, Summer 1986.

F Tomlinson's article 'What Do Women's Groups Offer?' in *Women in Management Review*, volume 2, number 4, Winter 1987.

DR JOHNSON HAS THE LAST WORD

The nuclear response

The ace up the network manager's sleeve is the response 'I don't know the answer, *but I know someone who does.*' This is the answer which justifies all the network manager's efforts to build up a network. This is the answer which demonstrates the awesome power of a well-managed network.

I began this book by sifting through various definitions of the word 'network', and quickly dismissed Dr Johnson's attempt as impressive, but not helpful. Let me make amends by allowing the doctor to have the final word on this subject. He was a networker's role model who gathered about him people with an astonishing range of knowledge and experience including Reynolds, the painter; Burke, the orator; Goldsmith, the poet; and Boswell, the biographer.

Boswell recorded Johnson's words about knowledge which all network managers should take to heart as we move towards the ascendency of the knowledge organisation:

> Knowledge is of two kinds: we know a subject ourselves, or we know where we can find information upon it.

Bibliography

Boe, A & Youngs, Bettie B (1989) *Is Your 'Net' Working?* John Wiley & Sons, Chichester

Customer Service Lead Body and Department of Employment (1993) *Customer Service Standards*, available from CSLB, Secretariat, Royal Mail, 132 Newport Road, Stafford ST16 1AA

Drucker, Peter (1993) *Post Capitalist Society* Butterworth Heinemann, Oxford

Handy, Charles (1994) *The Empty Raincoat*, Hutchinson, London

Institute of Careers Guidance and Centre for Research in Employment and Technology in Europe (1992) *1990s: Where Will The New Jobs Be?* Institute of Careers Guidance, 27A Lower High Street, Stourbridge, West Midlands DY8 1TA

Johnson, Dr (1816) *Dictionary* (11th ed), London

Kanter, Rosabeth Moss (1988) *The Change Masters* Unwin, London

Management Charter Initiative (MCI) and Department of Employment (1992) *Management Standards*, available from MCI, Russell Square House, 10–12 Russell Square, London WC1B 5BZ

Nakamoto, Michyo (1992) 'Japan and the European Community', *Financial Times*

Index

THIS BOOK IS FOR YOU IF YOU WANT TO:

- keep up with changes in your specialist area;
- sell something;
- work towards a National Vocational Qualification by managing a network;
- enlist support for a deserving cause;
- buy something;
- keep up with changes outside your specialist area;
- find a new job;
- recruit a business network manager;
- develop your career;
- contract out a service;
- exchange something;
- be a teleworker, away from the traditional office:
- bid for a service contract;
- maintain links with useful contacts;
- tap into new areas of knowledge;
- de-merge a conglomerate;
- use others to provide a benchmark for your own performance.

For all these activities, using the leverage of a **network** will give you a sustainable competitive advantage. But only if you manage your network properly.

This book will show you quickly what a network is, and how to manage it effectively.

It does not deal with TV networks, network diagrams for project management, computer networks, or rail networks.